Furniture
for Interior Design

Published in 2014
by Laurence King Publishing Ltd
361–373 City Road
London EC1V 1LR
Tel +44 20 7841 6900
Fax +44 20 7841 6910
E enquiries@laurenceking.com
www.laurenceking.com

A catalogue record for this book is available from the British Library

ISBN 978 1 78067 322 6
Design: John Round Design
Senior Editor: Peter Jones
Printed in China

Furniture
for Interior Design

Sam Booth and Drew Plunkett

Laurence King Publishing

Contents

Introduction

No furniture = no interior

Interior designers work within the shells of existing buildings, which are sometimes new but more frequently old and in need of adaptation to refresh tired aesthetics, create new identities and accommodate new functions. This book will explore the role of furniture in the process of that transformation of empty, underperforming shells. It will demonstrate the processes of designing, making and selecting furniture, and explore the strategies for its deployment.

The architect Norman Foster has said: 'Furniture is like architecture in microcosm.' As such, it must bear closer scrutiny than the exterior of any building because those who use it come, unavoidably, into direct visual and physical contact with it and are made more aware of its practical efficiency and of the aesthetic language it speaks.

The physical dimensions and aesthetic character of any building shell will, and should, influence the nature of a new interior inserted within it. Furniture will play a crucial – probably the most crucial – part in the refinement of the new installation and the physical interaction between interior elements and those who use them. It should comprehensively fulfil its practical obligation to support human activity without compromising efficiency or comfort, but it should also meet a less tangible obligation to stimulate and satisfy the aesthetic appetites of those who use it, regardless of how utilitarian or how hedonistic the activity it supports may be. While a designer must understand how to construct the major elements of walls, floors and ceilings, it is as important to master and refine the practical skills that

shape the miniaturized architectural language of furniture. However grand the conceptual intention, poor practical resolution will invite and deserve a negative response.

Form will be defined by function. Generic forms have evolved to serve, and enrich, the range of physical and intellectual human activities, and these are the rudiments of an aesthetic language that is shared by designers and those who use their work against which each new piece will be assessed. Chairs must be for sitting on. Tabletops must be horizontal. Dimensions will be determined by the limitations of the human body, and materials by the diverse degrees of use and abuse to which they are subjected. However, while it is comparatively easy to meet these prescribed practicalities, ultimately the success of a piece of furniture depends on its capacity to satisfy and stimulate the user's sensory experience. Its texture and temperature will be intimately experienced. It will affect the acoustic of the room in which it sits for good or ill. Its smell can pervade and characterize a room. It will make an impression on those who use it and they may well leave an impression on it.

From the simple utilitarian layout of plastic stacking chairs in an otherwise empty and characterless meeting place to pieces that go beyond conventional definitions and expectations to become something akin to sculpture or internal architecture, furniture inevitably communicates symbolic, aesthetic and cultural values. The reception desk in the entrance lobby of an office can encapsulate the status and intent of the business. The chairs in the

The functional element, the conventional, albeit grandiose, chair on which the emperor of China sat, mutates into an expression of divine status.

Left
A newly elected president selects a chair that is comfortable – and thereby implies a more democratic intent.

Above
The ubiquitous stacking chair is wholly egalitarian and has achieved its dominance because it works. It is easy to sit on, at least for a limited period, easily adapted to different activities, easily stored and comparatively easy on the eye.

lobby of a hotel can signal the quality of the experiences it offers. The service counter becomes the signature of a bar. The same empty space can be populated with different furniture pieces organized in different layouts and each variation will give it a different identity – formal or informal, practical or romantic, tranquil or vibrant, without making reference to the architecture of the original shell, other than to use it as a foil to intensify perception of the new.

Throughout the book the word 'furniture' will be used to describe any element that is functionally independent of the walls, floors and ceilings that enclose the space in which it sits. It may be built into walls or fixed to walls and floors for most of the furniture created by interior designers, other than project-defining set pieces, is intended to resolve the idiosyncracies of layouts and sites. Equal status will be accorded the one-off pieces and the wealth of manufactured options that are available and are specified rather than designed.

It is unlikely that designers will often have the opportunity, or obligation, to devote the time necessary to produce a successful piece in the pressurized design phase of the vast majority of interior projects; it is questionable whether it would always be appropriate to do so anyway. The complexities of designing something as apparently simple and familiar as a chair – the fine-tuning of dimensions and testing of the structure – demand their own expertise. Mass production of tried-and-tested pieces by specialist designers in specialist factories is, almost inevitably, more efficient and cost-effective. Throughout this book, mass-produced furniture will be described as 'specified', meaning that an

interior designer will choose pieces from a manufacturer's pre-existing range, specifying the model, finalizing options for materials and performance if necessary, and the number of pieces required. There are occasions when the particular needs of a project will justify the production of a small number of bespoke pieces, such as restaurant seating or shop display systems, and an interior designer can and should seize enthusiastically the opportunities they offer for creative speculation. The manufacture of pieces in limited numbers is classified as 'batch production' and the work is usually carried out, off site, in a specialist workshop.

Many of the elements that most emphatically establish the identity of an interior – bar counters and reception desks, hanging rails and display plinths – are unlikely to be available ready-made. Their size or their importance in creating identity demands that they be project-specific. Whether they generate or augment decisions about the whole, they should be compatible with the material palette of the walls, floor and ceiling, and with other pieces specified from manufacturers' catalogues. They need not be complex. Their detailing should be honed to clarify expression of the conceptual idea that underpins them and to simplify the processes of their production.

Before choosing to reinvent the chair or any other generic piece, a designer needs to be sure that his or her creation will be genuinely better than one that already exists and that, regardless of its visual qualities, its practical performance will meet its obligations. From Charles Rennie Mackintosh and Frank Lloyd Wright, through Ludwig Mies van der Rohe and Le Corbusier, to Philippe Starck and

Norman Foster, architects and designers have developed furniture intended for a specific interior that has gone on to be produced in volume and to find a life beyond that for which it was originally created. Most of these project-specific pieces have undergone subtle modifications to make them compatible with large-scale production. Some, designed and still prized for their visual qualities above all else, lack the simple, practical refinements that would make them natural choices for modest everyday use. The same designers when designing chairs intended for mass production from the outset have the ability to resolve the equation of style and comfort more successfully.

In the last fifty years, interior designers have increasingly moved beyond their traditional territory in the domestic sector to create public interiors, for leisure and retail businesses, and semi-private workplaces. This has encouraged and supported specialist furniture designers and the growth of manufacturing and retailing companies that find it profitable to specialize in one or more of these areas. Increased production has followed increased enthusiasm for interior design in private and public sectors and that growth spurt has been accelerated, in the last quarter of the twentieth century and into the twenty-first, by significant shifts in design philosophies.

The advent of Postmodernism in the late 1970s and early '80s undermined the primacy of High Modernism. Designers, of both interiors and furniture, began experimenting with forms that were generated more by subjective expression than objective application of process, the result of an acceptance that function is not just about practicality, which is comparatively easy to achieve, but about giving aesthetic pleasure. This willingness, on the part of designers, to create in a, perhaps more democratic, language, accessible to lay consumers, met with disapproval amongst the hard-line acolytes of Modernism but ultimately has prevailed

and consumers' enthusiasm for it is demonstrated in the universal success of IKEA and other more modestly sized chains, and single shops that have found their own niche.

Initially the historicism that underpinned Postmodernist theory encouraged what were primarily light-hearted reinterpretations of traditional archetypes. The scale of furniture offered a productive area for experimentation and the chair, as the most complex of the familiar forms, presented a particularly promising testing ground for the new ideas. The historicist wing was most assertive in North America and its theoretical protagonist, Robert Venturi, produced a series of flat-planed plywood chairs that parodied, with painted pattern, the forms and mouldings of the most recognizable and respectable historical styles. While Alessandro Mendini's colour-spotted 'Proust' armchair (see opposite) was probably the most monumental example of historicism there were other activists, also based in and around Milan, who generated a European version of an alternative contemporary aesthetic. The Memphis group, led by Ettore Sottsass, argued the need for a more democratic aesthetic and drew on the language of the coffee bar with its colourful plastic laminates. They shared with the North Americans a predisposition for pure geometry. In stylistic contrast but philosophical alignment to Memphis was a movement, epitomized by Mendini's 'animal' pieces for Studio Alchimia, which set out to give identities to furniture that drew on natural materials and form, purporting to touch something visceral in their audience. While North American historicism lost its impetus quickly – perhaps because it constrained designers' imaginations within the canons, however freely interpreted, of historical, primarily Classical, precedent – the Italian models offered greater freedom of expression and that found an enthusiastic market, particularly in the new design-led cafés, bars and restaurants that increasingly dominated the leisure sector throughout the 1980s and thereafter.

Far left
Alessandro Mendini's 'Proust' armchair caricatured traditional form but acknowledged its subversive intent by the 'pointillist' paint finish that melded fabric and frame.

Left
Starck's stackable chair has chrome back legs and a moulded plastic seat and front legs.

Artist: Starck, Philippe (b. 1949)
Title: Louis 20 Chair, 1991
Location: Museum of Modern Art (MoMA)
City: New York
Country: USA
Period/Style: Post 1945
Genre: Design
Note: Blown polypropylene and polished aluminum, 33 3/16 x 18 1/2 x 21 1/2' (84.3 x 47 x 54.6 cm), seat h. 18 3/8' (46.7 cm). David Whitney Collection, gift of David Whitney. Acc.n.: 52.2000
Credits: Digital image, The Museum of Modern Art, New York/Scala, Florence

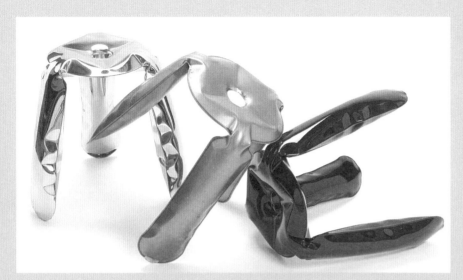

The potential of new technologies and the enthusiasm for sustainable design increasingly influences the way designers think. For their 'Plopp' range, Zieta Prozessdesign, have evolved a method of making objects from two sheets of ultra-thin and ultra-light steel, cut and welded by laser and inflated under high pressure, which gives strength, rigidity and stability to match those of the equivalent conventional pieces. The pieces may be inflated where and when required, reducing transportation costs and storage demands.

While die-hard Modernists loudly regretted the rejection of austere objectivity in favour of what they denounced as decorative frivolity, designers generally could not resist the new freedom for expression and experimentation and their output quickly found an enthusiastic audience of buyers that had eluded Modernists. The potency of the new furniture was given aesthetic and, more significantly, economic credibility with Philippe Starck's 1982 Café Costes in Paris and its eponymous chair. This three-legged, plywood, leather and metal piece perfectly complemented his historically referential interior without any overt borrowings from precedent. Its extraordinary form captured designers' and enough lay imaginations to precipitate the torrent of Starck furniture that followed. Quickly, other designers took inspiration from his redefinition of generic forms and took advantage of the market enthusiasm for furniture's more agreeable Postmodern face.

Starck moved on to transform the vocabulary of hotel design but crucial to each of the exemplars he presented was its bespoke furniture. There were several distinctive pieces in every project, each of which asserted its own identity but contributed to a complex but coherent whole. There can be few interior designers who do not, at some point, consider a Starck chair for their projects and they are now as common in chain restaurants as they once were in luxury hotels.

The subsequent significant changes that followed the fundamental stylistic shift to Postmodernism related to production processes rather than style. Digital design linked to digital manufacture evolved at the same time as a growing concern for sustainability. Furniture can have little or no effect on the environmental performance of a building and only choice of materials, cost of production and transportation costs will have bearing on the design decisions. Proliferating legislation protects materials and the environments in which they were harvested.

While digital design would encourage more elaborate proposals – and therefore more costly in terms of materials

and production – it could also be used to minimize material waste. Once programmed with data about the configuration of units to be produced, CNC (computer numerical control) machines (see p.120) automatically calculate the cutting pattern necessary to maximize the number of units that can be culled from source materials, and each unit can be unique without adding to cost or time.

Reuse and recycling, however, present the most obviously sustainable response to the problem – providing the processes do not use excessive amounts of energy. There are published guidelines from a number of reputable sources but, given the comparatively recent emergence of the subject, advice frequently changes and what was considered good practice is supplanted. The internet provides a comprehensive and generally reliable source of information.

Another relevant and increasingly significant area of concern is that relating to 'Universal' or 'Inclusive' design. Both are dedicated, primarily, to making buildings usable by as broad a spectrum of people, with or without disabilities, as possible. To a degree, the same priorities should apply to furniture design. Obviously furniture layouts are critical, to allow easy passage for wheelchair users and the semi-ambulant. When designing chairs, one should consider how users, particularly the old, can lower themselves into and rise from them. Colours are a crucial consideration for the visually impaired. Legislation principally covers buildings but the principles are ones that should also be embraced by all designers of furniture.

Designing is a collaborative process involving the client, the maker and other consultants; that collaboration can, and should, be a source of inspiration and pleasure. Searching for, finding and specifying existing pieces that complement an overall vision is an opportunity to collaborate, albeit vicariously, with every designer who has ever sketched a first tentative idea and nurtured it to realization. Online catalogues present the designer with an extraordinary range of choice, but the right search words produce an instant shortlist of familiar and unfamiliar options including the necessary information about performance and price that can clinch a choice. There is, however, no substitute for trying out the piece at first hand – actually sitting on the chair, leaning on the table – to test for comfort and efficiency.

The walls, floors, ceilings and openings that define the nature of a space also define the limits within which a designer may think and create. First inclinations will inevitably be to redefine boundaries significantly, subdividing or connecting, knocking down or knocking through, treating the existing building as a blank canvas on which to make grand, perhaps grandiloquent, gestures. More often, however, the opportunity to remove existing elements is not on offer. Some buildings will be legally protected because of their architectural merit or simply because their age makes them a crucial contribution to their location. There are also times when the existing building shell, although not officially protected, has qualities and elements that the designer may wish to incorporate into the new. For other projects, financial priorities can rule out an extended construction period, particularly in competitive commercial environments where high rents and local taxes require that trading begin as soon as possible. With short-term rentals, clients may hope to transport pre-existing fixtures and fittings to new premises. At the other extreme,

in the most competitive commercial sectors, businesses need to reposition themselves at regular intervals, to keep pace with rivals and to assert their continuing relevance to their target customer group. Commercial interiors tend to have a lifespan of about five years. For all these scenarios, furniture pieces, large and small, which are easily transportable, offer a solution and the most viable way to transfer identity between premises or redefine the character of existing spaces. Modestly sized furniture pieces that constitute the brand identity of multiple outlets are more easily accommodated within the diversity of available shells than are the large-scale gestures of new walls and levels.

Furniture, whether one-off or batch-production (a limited series of identical pieces), allows a designer to explore and experiment with forms, materials and methods of manufacture, unrestrained by the established practices and preferences of the mainstream building trade. As new digital techniques have revolutionized the way furniture is made and the technology used to explore and resolve ideas is becoming increasingly compatible with that used to programme the machines that translate them into reality, so designers' intentions can be communicated and implemented with the click of a mouse. There is no longer a need for makers to interpret instructions and negotiate compromises acceptable to designers. Digital machines have no preference for the

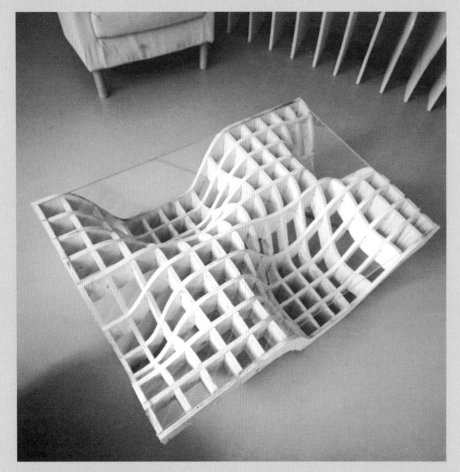

Left
CNC techniques allow complex and unique elements, each with slots for interlocking joints, to be cut with perfect precision. The accuracy of the process ensures that the points on the ribs for the support of the glass tabletop are in exact level alignment.

Left
In this bar the same technique as with the table on this page enables the plywood ceiling ribs to share form and material with wall fins and supports for the bar and shelf.

simple and the repetitive, and no fear of the complex and singular. Prototyping and batch production have become economically feasible for the most modest projects.

The argument made against computer-aided design and computer-aided manufacture by those wedded to the notion that creativity is dependent on hand-drawing and hand-making was that it produced uniformity of design, but designers can now better realize their individual inspirations and those who truly understand the capacity of digital technologies for both the conception and realization of ideas can explore forms that were, rightly and recently, regarded as unrealistic.

The acceleration of technological innovation is also providing a cornucopia of new materials and composites. The materials database Material ConneXion claims to add 50 to 60 new materials to its library each month, some so experimental that a use has still to be found for them. Ambitious designers should aim to keep up. It will often be immediately obvious that some innovations will be useful additions to their visual vocabularies. Others should be filed in the memory for recall when prompted by the particularities of a future project.

New ideas are not exclusively derived from the output of the high-tech or petrochemical industries. Concern for sustainability has given impetus to the search for renewable and organic-based composites and with that has come a revival of interest in traditional materials and methods of manufacture. Traditional is more likely to be local and local is more likely to be sustainable. It is no longer a contradiction to use state-of-the-art technology to process traditional materials or traditional artisanal techniques to work new materials.

Digital technologies have also fundamentally transformed in a few decades, and seem bent on further transforming, ways of living and working and, consequently, have led to the reinterpretation of familiar furniture pieces and new ways of deploying them. The typewriter that replaced the pen was displaced by the desktop computer that is now being usurped by the laptop and the entire content and operation of an office may be fitted on the touch-screen of the instrument that has evolved from, and still retains the increasing anachronistic label of, 'telephone'.

The first keyboard writing instruments were operated by full-time specialists (typists) but the words they typed were composed by someone else, someone without the time to master the machine well enough to avoid mistakes that could not then be invisibly mended. The process demanded skills that, although not easy to acquire, were not highly regarded.

The first computers offered those who composed the words the means to commit them to screen for consideration and then to paper. Few of the new computer users acquired typing techniques that matched those of the dedicated typists but mistakes could be made to disappear without trace and immediacy compensated for sloppy technique. Word processing machinery began to dominate the office desk and, before wireless connections, cable management was a crucial concern. The dedicated typist disappeared or assumed a new role, coping with the acceleration of administrative tasks that were generated by accelerated production of information.

Laptops have more capacity than the first desktops and may be taken and used anywhere. They incorporate in a compact shell a battery of unprecedented creative, communication and research tools. They are changing the definition of a working day and a working place.

The smart phone and the tablet further miniaturize, and fuse, the workplace and the social sphere. The workplace remains a locus for motivational and creative direct personal interaction, albeit in the face of digitally delivered distractions. Traditional person-to-person social interaction is increasingly conducted in the expectation that it will be communicated to, and scrutinized by, others on social networking sites. Perhaps paradoxically, that scrutiny demands that events should be conducted in contexts (interiors) that flatter the participant and impress the scrutineer.

Clockwise from top left
A mechanical typewriter, which, because it was unforgiving of errors, needed a skilled operator.

An early desktop computer, which, with its keyboard and mouse wiring and printer, required more work surface than a typewriter.

Each iteration of personal computing redefines how the mechanisms of life are conducted.

The portability and wireless connectivity of the laptop blurred boundaries between work and recreation, office and home.

Predigital/postdigital

In homes, the furniture that once filled rooms to accommodate cumbersome entertainment systems with multiple wirings has become redundant, replaced by personal, pocket-sized devices and wall-hung televisions that are as thin as paintings. The opportunities offered to individuals to fine-tune their recreation and to create private spaces, which are as likely to be made by earphones as they are by four walls, do not necessarily need new interpretations of conventional furniture pieces but, inevitably, these will evolve, just as different cooking techniques, fast food and slow food, new ingredients and ways of eating from around the globe have changed the rituals of eating in the home and the landscapes of restaurants.

Good furniture design has always added an appropriate aesthetic dimension to the end products of ergonomic and anthropometric data. In the last few decades digital technology's precipitous redefinition of all aspects of human conduct suggests that a definitive conclusion must soon be reached but history instead demonstrates that, while change may decelerate, it is constant and will continually present challenges and opportunities to designers. While the grammar of how spaces are used is changing, designers might be wise to draw on and add the lessons of cultural histories and the communal consensus to their interpretation of new technologies and materials. Technological innovation offers possibilities and the designer's role is to find ways to exploit and maximize a potential that was unanticipated by those who made the technological innovation but the result can only be validated by those who may choose to use it.

Inspiration is becoming more eclectic and stylistic options are becoming greater, but the process of design – dependent on human creativity – remains constant. It involves taking an idea that exists as an abstraction and finding a way to make it a reality. Ideas come from seeing, touching or otherwise experiencing something that triggers the first imaginative impulse, even if the original source is far removed from the ultimate intent. It is probably true that the further the final outcome has moved from the first manifestation, the better it will be, because it has been subjected to and shaped by progressive waves of analysis and criticism. Designers cannot allow themselves to be solely subjective. They have an obligation to their client, and their client's clients and customers, which means that their ideas must be tempered by objective assessment of what will elicit appropriate responses from users. This is as true for the interior designers in the public sector as it is for those in the most competitive private realms.

A home office expresses its occupant's preferences and priorities more precisely than a shared space.

A designer's priority should always be to refine visually the essential practical underpinning of any interior and the furniture it contains. The aesthetic qualities that make this visual veneer successful depend on an ability to control the making process and that comes from being able to recognize, evolve and explain a conceptual idea, and to understand how to orchestrate the functional and aesthetic potential of different materials and technologies. The crucial skill is knowing not how to construct every conceivable joint or understanding the applications of every material, but how to see the inherent possibilities in them and to be fluent in the visual and verbal languages necessary to ask questions of and communicate intentions to those who have the practical skills and experience to realize such possibilities. Designers do not need to know how to operate a machine or use a tool. In fact, it is usually better that they do not try because, if techniques and skills are not practised daily, it is better they are not used at all. Unpractised makers will be slower and their output less refined. Rather, designers need to know what a machine or a tool can do and to respect the practical expertise and knowledge of the makers, and to take advice from them and build on it.

The importation of sushi to the West, and with it conveyor-belt service, has changed the way food is selected and upgraded the status of the service counter. Self-service has become glamorous and its mechanisms have prompted, in this example, thinking about how best to accommodate chopsticks and other paraphernalia in slots that discourage their dissemination across the counter.

Case study 'Tip Ton' chair

Above
'Tip Ton', a chair that stacks – and rocks.

Left and far left
The chair leans forwards with the user.

This is an example of how the perceptive reconsideration of how people really use chairs, can lead to significant reconfiguration of something as universally familiar as the stacking chair and how a refined eye can translate that reappraisal to produce something of beauty. The leap of perception that inspired the 'Tip Ton' chair demonstrates that it is possible to reinvent the wheel – or the stacking chair.

The premise behind the idea is that when people are listening, reading or relaxing they sit back, and when they are working or eating they lean forwards. This has been rationalized into a chair that stacks but has some of the kinetic capacity of a rocking chair. Stacking chairs cannot incorporate the refinements that make good work chairs, but the Tip Ton is particularly suited to classrooms and meetings in which users sit back and listen and lean forwards to write. That it is extremely beautiful, gaining from the inevitable comparisons with the overly familiar stacking polypropylene shell on spindly metal legs, prompts the thought that the rational analysis that generated the concept also gave it a clarity of form that needed no superfluous embellishment.

PART 1 CONTENT AND CONTEXT

Content and context

Whether they are working speculatively or to commission, furniture designers will have in mind a context for each piece they produce and that perception is crucial in decision-making. An office chair is necessarily different from a dining chair, which necessarily differs from an armchair. Designers creating a project-specific piece will have a clear perception of its precise context and functional content but whether they create all, some or none of the furniture used in a particular project, their responsibility is to orchestrate the deployment of individual pieces so that each gives meaning to, and takes significance from its place in, the ensemble. Old pieces may be counterpointed by new. Pieces that are magnificent in isolation may not contribute as much to the whole as more modest options.

Interior designers should not gratuitously design pieces when tried-and-tested, factory-made options exist but, to take advantage of that abundance of choice, they need to have a comprehensive awareness of what is on offer. There will always be a tendency to favour a limited collection of preferred pieces but, since furniture is so crucial to the success of the singular interior it occupies, repetitive selection should be questioned.

The content of an interior will be established by the client or by the client in discussion with the designer, whose responsibility it is to organize space efficiently, as an armature on which to lay the aesthetic veneers of finishes and furniture. Clumsy planning can devalue aesthetic intent. Efficient planning can reduce overheads, improve productivity and establish the aesthetic balance, but there is no simple set of rules that may be applied across the spectrum of interiors. Fine-tuning

of basic layout principles will deliver more effective solutions. As long as decisions to adapt are not made gratuitously, adjustments will generally be for the better.

There are a number of books, such as Tutt and Adler's *The New Metric Handbook* and Packard's *The Architect's Handbook*, that give dimensional data about furniture sizes and planning layouts. While such books provide valuable reference information, they are most useful for the design of new buildings when the dimensions and plan form may be readily adjusted to suit the prescribed data. With existing interior spaces, however, planning is usually less straightforward. Existing plans are unlikely to accommodate prescribed layouts. It will normally be necessary to decide how much recommended dimensions may be trimmed without prejudicing practicalities. Frequently, if the precise nature of the activity to be accommodated is objectively analysed it may be possible to reduce the recommended allocation for individuals, or to accept that it must be exceeded. The general rules have a factor of safety that can be judiciously pared. Overly rigorous pruning will result in humiliation for the designer.

Designers should take comfort from the knowledge that awkward sites and the problems they pose encourage more ingenious design thinking. It is also important to remember that raw data does not take into consideration how users will experience it in context. The singular beauty of any piece of furniture will go unappreciated if its deployment makes those who use it physically uncomfortable or psychologically uneasy.

Different layouts may encourage or discourage communication and collaboration between workers

Above
The human body seldom conforms to the generalities of anthropometric and ergonomic guidelines.

Right
Standard data is an excellent starting point for planning layouts but the dimensions of an existing interior space will seldom conform to the suggested layouts.

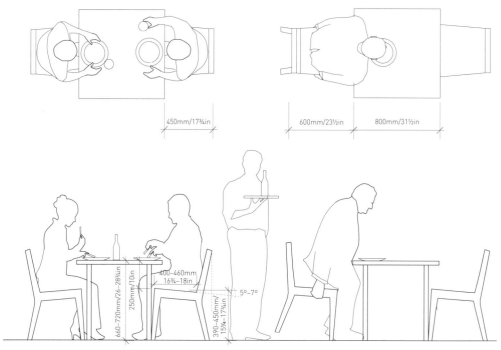

and determine the nature and degree of interaction in social contexts. Decisions about the desirability of a particular kind of layout can be made from observation of how existing environments function and by questioning those who use them, but ultimately, like all good design, success depends on a designer's intuition. The most extraordinary conceptual proposal will be worthless if it fails to perform practically. Users may find it difficult to articulate their objections to aesthetic gestures but they are well equipped to criticize practical shortcomings and will seize on the latter to undermine concepts to which they take exception.

Generic contexts

The unique considerations that relate to the provision of furniture within different categories of interiors and are worth listing. The points cited in the following passage relate primarily to practical considerations but ultimately pieces specified or designed must respond to the character of the organization they serve. All categories of building have been affected by the shifts in habits and behaviour precipitated by digital technologies. So profound have those changes been that it is easy to forget that, while the first widespread manifestations of change emerged in the last decade of the last century, it is only in this century that the influence has accelerated and the impact been fundamentally significant. It is an interesting time to be reconsidering familiar furniture typologies and the interiors they defined.

In workplaces, the consequences of general technological progress have been evident for a couple of centuries. It immediately changed the way in which people worked but, until recently, production remained labour-intensive. Digitally enhanced production methods now need fewer and different kinds of people, and digital communication has created new kinds of jobs and prompted new ways of working. The computer, whether desktop or laptop, allows the person who composes the content of a letter to make it legible. It allows a designer to make 'drawings' on the same machine that is used to research the information needed to make them real. Digital information transmission means that underperforming postal services are no longer an excuse for poor communication.

As the capacity of digital technology has become greater, so its physical packaging has become increasingly miniaturized. The realities of mobility now affect the nature of all the pieces of furniture that have evolved to support sedentary activities. Functional zoning has remained recognizably constant and the furniture within zones still broadly fulfils its traditional functional obligations but as the new social media erode social boundaries and discredit formality, physical separation becomes more permeable and furniture layouts are increasingly used to define dedicated areas. The need to express individual or corporate identity looks increasingly to interiors as one of the means to articulate identity, and to furniture as a crucial component in fine-tuning that declaration.

The sections that follow set out the fundamental considerations when specifying or designing furniture for each of the generic categories of interior and the discrete spaces and activities they house.

Below

Different table types and orientations can affect preferred dimensions. While the variation introduced by a single table is modest, the accumulated effect of multiple tables is often significant. Projections or indentations on a plan can cause localized problems.

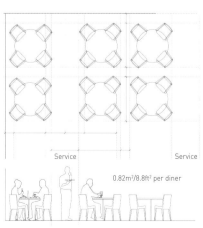

Service   Service

0.82m²/8.8ft² per diner

Round

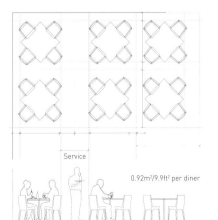

Service

0.92m²/9.9ft² per diner

Diagonal

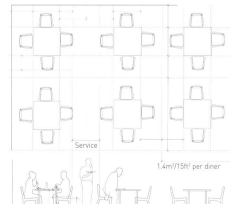

Service

1.4m²/15ft² per diner

Square

Case study Better planning solves problems

Research, and personal experience, suggest that efficient planning is not enough to make a good interior. Users have to enjoy being in it, and for this they will be prepared to accept a degree of functional compromise. This principle applies across the spectrum of interior environments but is perhaps most likely to be overlooked in workplaces, where pleasure has, understandably, been seen as of secondary importance. But, since work is a primary source of self-esteem, the right choice of furniture will have a benign effect. An intelligent response to the existing elements of an interior is necessary to maximize the effectiveness of furniture. In the example illustrated the client had brought furniture from his old to his new office and, finding the working environment unsatisfactory, had called for professional advice.

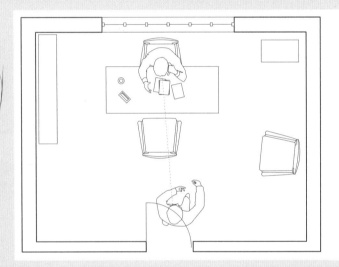

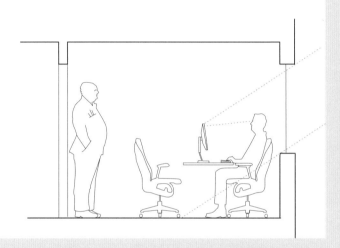

Above
In the office shown above, the client sits with his back to the window. Light shines on his computer screen; he blocks light from his work surface; he is aware that interesting things may be happening beyond the window; and when visitors enter he and they are immediately confrontational.

Below
With the new layout shown below, his problems with light and reflection are solved; he can glance out of the window when curious; he has a more informal first encounter with visitors, who will be impressed when confronted by the very desirable view from the window.

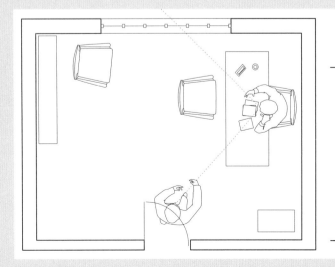

Retail

It is generally held that furniture in shops, whether for product display or customer comfort, should modestly complement the merchandise on offer. While the principle owes something to designers' predilection for minimalism, it also makes practical sense. Display systems that are too complex can be difficult for customers to access and staff to tidy and service. In a modest shop with dense displays, the ratio of staff to customers will be low. In more expensive shops, the ratio will be high and staff will have time to curate and look after displays.

The lifespan of most retail interiors is short, seldom more than five years, and this is particularly true for high-street chains and most prevalent in fashion retail, where looks count and businesses compete to declare their serial newness. More expensive shops tend to invest more, to make a statement about brand rather than product, and branding is less likely to be casually tinkered with, because its message will be more fundamental to identity.

Below
A retail interior should assert its presence but furniture should play second fiddle to the merchandise.

Below
More modestly scaled products
may justify more flamboyant
furniture to draw custom.

In shop design there are simple, proven maxims that retailers abide by that must be respected by designers.

Layout strategy is fundamentally important and can influence the detailed design of individual pieces. Control of customer circulation, particularly in densely packed interiors, is important to ensure their exposure to the full range of merchandise. Display in more expensive shops is more sparse and the whole interior tends to be visible from the moment of entry. Location of counters and pay points should also be considered strategically. Placed at the entrance, they suggest, and deliver, control. Further into the body of the shop they allow customers to enter and browse without pressure from sales assistants. When counters are free of the obligation to display products, they offer an opportunity for brand identity.

Signals given by expensive fittings and finishes deter those without adequate funds; shoppers free from financial concerns will read the same signals as confirmation of quality. Secure display systems present more complex problems. Once the width of a counter, often itself doubling as a display cabinet, and with an assistant was a primary deterrent, distancing potential thieves from the drawers and open shelves behind it. The

counter as barrier has necessarily disappeared in self-service shops but remains, partly as a security barrier, in shops selling smaller, higher-value products. Other items, secured in impenetrable glass cases on the sales floor, allow customers, accustomed to less formal shopping rituals, to browse before confronting staff and committing to buy.

The counter is increasingly being removed, even in shops selling the most expensive luxury goods. It offers limited defence against criminals motivated to extreme measures by high-value goods. Its removal is also an acknowledgement that the personal and empathetic attention of a sales assistant, without the barrier of a counter, can consolidate a sale. Serious discussions about expensive purchases are now more likely to be conducted at elegant tables in generously proportioned rooms with specific items brought as required from secure storage. Glass is the ubiquitous material for display cabinets and transparency presents designers with interesting opportunities to find solutions that complement the products while incorporating the mechanisms of drawer runners, hinges and alarm systems. Smooth operation implies perfection. The small scale of luxury items, like jewellery and watches, requires the display zone to be concentrated at eye level and the structure that supports or contains it is therefore particularly significant. Display furniture in any retail area must be stable. A hanging rail should not sag under the weight of the garments it displays and a shelving unit should not tremble when customers remove items for closer scrutiny.

Above left
Evidence of security precautions enhances the perceived value of expensive merchandise.

Above right
Often the particularities of a site will prompt a one-off gesture. Here the serpentine bench that coils around existing columns provides seating for customers trying on shoes and contrasts with the straight glass shelves that line the perimeter.

Shelving as Wall, Ceiling and Branding Image
Baker D. Chirico – March Studio

Bread shops, particularly those offering traditionally baked goods, necessarily have a quick turnover of product. This interior, with its wooden shelving and counter, and the patina of its plastered wall, suggests appropriately artisanal values, while the stainless-steel oven behind the mirrored wall indicates good hygienic standards. The three-dimensional complexity of the shelving wall and ceiling is only feasible with CNC technology.

Above
Bulging profiles and irregular lengths of shelving suggest the form and texture of rustic loaves. The mitred corners of the counter top timbers allow them to wrap up the front's horizontal strips. Digital scales and the till screen are set in to the counter top.

Below
CNC cutting produces the components that interlock to form the shelving/wall/ceiling structure. The more conventional timber strips of the counter top and front emulate the linearity of the shelves.

Below left
Axonometric
1   15mm/½in CNC-cut plywood panels.
2   Existing masonry wall.
3   9mm/¼in CNC-cut plywood ribs.
4   2no.* 240 x 45mm/9½ x 1¾in hanging
    beam fixed to joists above.

* This is standard notation, meaning that
there will be two of the piece described.

Below right
Section
1   Angle cleat connection of rib to masonry.
2   2no.* 240 x 45mm/9½ x 1¾in
    hanging beam fixed to joists above.
3   Steel connector.
4   Front face of panel joint.
5   Rear face of panel joint.
6   2no. 15mm/½in CNC-cut and
    perforated plywood panels.
7   Front face of panel joint.
8   Rear face of panel joint.
9   Angle cleat bolted to masonry and plywood.

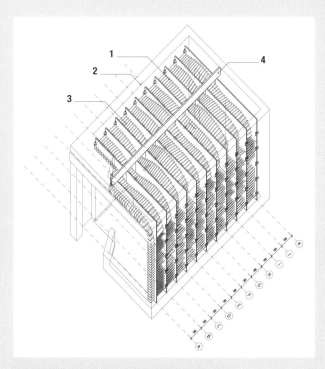

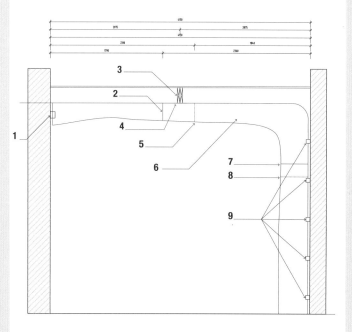

Right
CNC cutting schedule.
The profile of individual vertical and horizontal
elements is plotted digitally on a standard
sheet of plywood, to minimize waste.
1   15mm/½in verticals.
2   19mm/¾in ceiling.
3   19mm/¾in shelves.

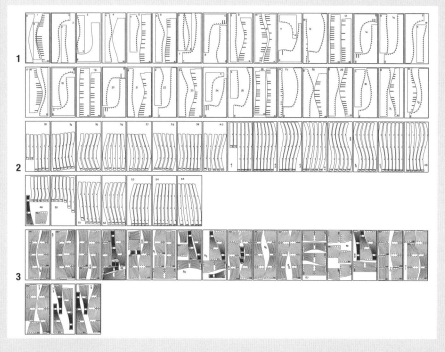

Three legs are less steady than four, and suspended structures will sway with the slightest provocation. Since most businesses operate in rented premises, it is seldom permissible or financially desirable to bolt legs to floors or find secure fixings for suspension wires in ceilings. Damage to existing structures has to be made good. Radical solutions cannot afford to be impractical failures. An idea, however seductive, that cannot be translated into a viable reality will look like – and will be – a designer's folly.

Wiring for light sources and alarms is comparatively easy to hide within the body of shelving or cabinet construction but the availability of power sources in existing premises will have a bearing on the location of display furniture. It is simple to plan for ideal socket positions but in existing premises it may be necessary to find discreet surface-mounted routes for cabling. For shelves and storage units on perimeter walls, it is usually possible to find an arrangement of furniture that will provide the necessary cover. For open displays on freestanding shelves and plinths, a general light level from ceiling-mounted fittings, with pendant lights or spotlights for product-specific illumination, can provide an adequate level. Light sources, particularly spotlights, can be reflected and cause glare on glass cases. It is better if they are concealed within the structure of the cabinet, to cast light directly on products without shining into shoppers' eyes. The solid structure of cabinets or shelves should be deep enough to accommodate the selected

fittings, usually small spotlights or thin tubes, and include ventilation openings to avoid overheating. Spotlights are typically fixed into the top of a cabinet and tubes to a solid strip on the top edge of the glazed front so that light is directed away from customers and down to the product.

Expensive specialist shops will need the services of a designer to deliver the sort of interior that can serve as a leading element in their visual 'branding'. Modest businesses are more likely to turn to suppliers who offer generic storage and display solutions.

Designers will normally use specialist contractors for the manufacture and installation of project-specific pieces. Such shopfitting companies will have specialist workshops. It is normal practice for designers to supply them with drawings setting out dimensions and specifying materials, and for the workshops to produce their own, more detailed construction drawings, compatible with their machinery and techniques. They will present these to the designer for checking to ensure that the finished product will meet the aesthetic intention. The nature of this collaboration puts an onus on the shopfitting company to take responsibility for quality of making, and they may also carry out the installation since their site team's experience of their own products and techniques is likely to enable them to deal more effectively with problems that arise on site. This streamlining of process is important in reducing installation time. When existing premises are being refurbished, it is normal for shopfitters

to work between the end of trade on one day and the start of business on the next, thereby endeavouring to reduce non-trading, non-profit-making time to a minimum.

Not all furniture and fittings need be bespoke. There are comprehensive ranges of manufactured items and, for small businesses with modest turnovers, these will normally be the most feasible solution. They can be customized to suit the identity of a particular business but need to be finished to a standard that matches the originals. Detailing of cheap bespoke pieces is better kept simple, so that it may be executed to a high standard at minimal cost.

Rents, loans and local taxes must be paid as soon as possession of empty premises begins and will continue to be paid while on-site work is carried out. The finely tuned economics of retailing mean that speed of installation is important so that trading and income generation can begin as soon as possible. It is normal for furniture fabrication to be carried out off site. This also ensures better quality. Access is not usually a problem given that shops tend to open directly onto a street.

Specialist shopfitting has a comparatively long history and the better companies involved have their own streamlined production and installation techniques. They will often also be responsible for installing new wall surfaces, which offers the opportunity for the productive integration of finished wall and display system. It is normal practice for designers to send drawings specifying the dimensions and materials of proposed pieces to shopfitting companies, which will make production drawings particular to their own processes. These will then be sent back to the designer for approval before making begins.

Larger-scale businesses can aspire to their own ranges of product-specific furniture and fittings, often as expressions of national and international brand identity. More specialist chains find expression of identity easier but, since they are obliged to inhabit a diverse range of shells, from the bland rectilinear volumes of shopping malls to the awkward idiosyncratic plans and low ceilings of historically significant buildings, furniture is generally scaled modestly to allow flexible planning.

Luxury chains, or single luxury shops, tend to express their status with expensive materials and precise detailing. They will tend to display fewer objects, as an outcome and expression of the unique qualities of the products they offer. Provision for customers will be generous. Counters for paying and tables for wrapping are likely to be located discreetly and sometimes entirely out of sight.

Opposite
Sparse display is matched by minimal display furniture.

Right
Display furniture should be self-effacing to merchandise but should match it in quality.

Far right
The rational construction of this freestanding unit is underlined by equal division of the end elevation and the frameless insertion of the glass into the centre joint and ceiling. The plinth, which protects the vulnerable bottom edges from abrasive damage also raises the sharp straight bottom edges to prevent their being visually compromised by the uneven surface of the carpet. All floor surfaces are uneven to some degree and it is therefore always good practice to separate them visually from the nominal bottom edge of a piece of furniture.

Hanging rails

Hanging rails are ubiquitous in clothes shops, whether they are budget, luxury or any of the gradations between. They offer the most compact way of storing and displaying products while making them easily accessible to browsing customers. Cheaper shops often overload rails. More expensive shops hang more sparsely because they carry more limited stock, to signal comparative exclusivity and, frequently, to conform to the minimalist aesthetic they favour.

Garments are usually 'side hung', that is with the hanger at right angles to the rail. Provision is sometimes made for 'front hanging' in which single garments,

usually typical of those side hung on the same rail, are displayed more effectively. The normal technique for front hanging is to project the rail beyond the upright so that the rail has a notch or slight upward projection to hold the hook of a hanger in place. Expensive shops seldom use front hanging because their sparse hanging makes examination of individual garments comparatively simple.

Hanging rails are usually simple metal structures with components welded or bolted together. Stability is most simply provided by base rails at right angles to the length.

Above left
Base rails at right angles to the hanging rail provide stability and the wheels refine what would otherwise be a prosaic junction with the floor – while dealing better with the inevitable unevennesses in the floor.

Left
A folded metal allusion to stairs in the basement of a shoe shop.

Above
Hanging rails do not have to be modest. Here beaten metal fascias mask rails and shelves for handbags.

A Connecting Line
Custo – Dear Design

While graphic imagery, which may be changed frequently with minimal interruption, offers the simplest way to establish identity and presence on high streets and in shopping malls, furniture pieces offer opportunities for more permanent, perhaps less assertive, expressions of branding.

In this shop, the first international outlet for a Spanish fashion chain, linear horizontality provides an assertive identity.

Left
Metal rails may be easily shaped. Here the curve relates to the ceiling moulding.

Below
Construction of hanging rails can be, and usually is, simple; metal tubes with bolted, screwed or welded joints. In this stainless-steel example the short length, at ninety degrees to the main length, allows 'front hanging' of garments, for more effective display. Side hanging allows more storage that is directly accessible to customers.

Above
The projecting splayed MDF shelves appear to be sandwiched for support between the slightly convex strips but are cantilevered from the wall.

Above right
The outline of the wall-leaning mirror shares the angles of the plinth and counter.

Right
Floor- and wall-mounted elements are characterized by stacked layers of MDF painted white. The logo font shares their stretched horizontality. Plinths and counter, angled in the horizontal and vertical planes, relate to the ceiling structure.

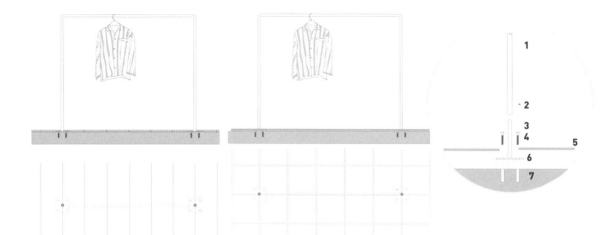

Below
Chair shells and a wall, customized with fabric swathes and duplicated in a wall-sized mirror, stamp identity on a modest rectangular room.

Above left
The tubular rail is welded to thin base plates, which are bolted to the subfloor and the floor finish is laid over them. With tiles or timber flooring, it is preferable if the junction between floor and rail occurs on a joint to maintain the suggestion of precision. The thickness of grout or underlay can match that of the base plate.

Above and above right
The alternative, which is most useful where a monolithic floor finish is specified, involves the sliding of the hollow rail over a section of similar profile welded to a base plate, which is bolted to the subfloor. The outer sleeve covers any irregularities in the screed where the inner tube emerges. It is fixed securely with a set screw. With a tile finish, it is preferable for the tube to emerge at the junction of four tiles to make cutting easier.

1 Hanging rail.
2 Set screw.
3 Inner tube.
4 Expansion bolts to fix plate to subfloor.
5 Floor finish (monolithic screed, timber or tiles).
6 Metal plate pre-drilled for bolts.
7 Subfloor.

Reception areas

Roles and interactions within offices and public buildings have changed but the importance of the reception area, which presents the first and best opportunity for an organization to express its status and ethos, is undiminished. Some businesses and institutions will choose to convey serious intent and formality, others something more amenable. There are a few off-the-shelf options available but it is usual for the reception desk to be unique to the company and its space. Normally the bigger the company, the bigger the reception space and the desk will be proportionally substantial, fulfilling a rhetorical role, impressing visitors and reminding employees of the nature of the company for which they work. It can inspire pride or encourage cynicism, if its grandiloquence implies qualities it does not deliver.

The number of people working behind a desk at one time, which is determined by the traffic it must handle at peak times, will decide its functional length but a front elevation may be stretched to increase its presence. A generous length of worktop also helps to keep the area behind the desk front, which is visible to visitors, uncluttered, which suggests efficiency.

The placing of the desk is important, to avoid the impression of confrontation between visitor and receptionist. While the desk should be the first thing visitors see, it is appropriate to have some distance, and a few metres will do, between desk and door so that visitors have a brief time to assess the environment and the receptionist before the first direct interaction. In a shallow entrance area the desk to one side of the entrance eliminates immediate confrontation. Just as the desk should be proportional to the space containing it, a modest component in a modest space, so scale of detail is important. Intimidating bulk can be deconstructed into sections that relate to different functions. A high front section, wide enough to support bags and packages, visually shields the working surface, the equipment it carries and the storage beneath it. The raised front serves as a surface against which a visitor may lean comfortably when talking to the receptionist, may fill forms and sign documents. The rear of the upstand, usually open to the worktop, provides storage.

Reception desks are not generally required to resist heavy or abusive use and choice of materials is guided more by aesthetic considerations than practicalities.

An assertive reception desk can make a strong statement about the organization it fronts.

Materials need to look pristine throughout the life of the desk, given that it is the first expression of an organization's ethos. Hard and hard-edged materials predominate, partly because they make a more effective transition between a building's exterior and its softer interior and, more prosaically because they are less vulnerable to modest wear. Areas likely to receive heavier wear may generally be identified at the design stage and provision may be made by substitution of more resilient materials at those points.

The extent of work carried out by receptionists will depend on the activity and structure of the organization they front. For some the role will be full-time, for others, whose responsibility will also include administrative or secretarial tasks, it will not necessarily be the most time-consuming part of their job. Some, particularly in the latter group, will work sitting down. Others who require to be more mobile, like those consistently consulting paper-based records, will be more efficient with a surface suitable for working while standing with occasional access to a stool. Standing receptionists and those sitting on stools or chairs on a raised floor area have better eye contact with visitors.

Wiring for power distribution and communication systems was once a major consideration in desk design but the frequent combination of the receptionist's role and that of company telephonist has all but disappeared. For most organizations modest desktop switchboard devices have been replaced by the telephone's own keypad and workers have direct telephonic communication within the office and the world beyond. Now the receptionist need only cope with general enquiries and requires no more telephonic equipment than any other worker. Wireless connections have eliminated most of the cabling associated with computers.

Reception areas tend to be well lit, often with generous natural light from glazed entrance doors, but most desks will require some additional localized lighting for both workers and visitors, either from a high level of artificial lighting over the desk or dedicated task lighting. Isolated pools of task lights can significantly increase the glamour of a reception area. Standard lights may be fixed on desktops when they can fulfil the secondary role of defining work positions. Lighting concealed in the soffit of a projecting top element can wash down the desk front. Lighting concealed behind it can provide task light for working areas. Lighting concealed in a toe recess can wash across a floor. The design maxim that physical characteristics and limitations of the given space should be made a virtue of suggests that lack of natural light should be treated positively and the desk and the space in which it stands defined in darker hues and more theatrical lighting.

The wall behind a reception desk should be considered part of the same composition.

Reception specifications

In cross section a reception desk will normally have a high front, to shield the equipment used by those who work behind it at a standard desk height and whose role frequently involves more than receiving and processing visitors. The raised front should shield as much evidence of mundane activity as possible. There should be a lower section to accommodate visiting wheelchair users and this can be a useful generator of form.

All reception desks should have a lower section, with a knee recess on the visitors' side (see below) to accommodate wheelchair users. Knee recesses for able-bodied workers will serve equally well for their wheelchair-bound colleagues. For ambulant visitors space must be made for feet as they stand against the desk front. This can take the form of a 'toe recess', usually about 100mm/4in high and 50mm/2in deep that also protects the base of the desk from kick damage. A recess has the additional advantage of disguising the uneven junction of the perfectly straight bottom edge of a desk and the, almost inevitably uneven, floor on which it sits. If the visual separation is minimized to allow the mass of the desk to rest directly on the floor then projection of the higher front section will provide the necessary toe space.

Below
1 Average reception desk/bar height.
2 Practical height for wheelchair and standing users.
3 Maximum height for oblique reach.
4 Maximum height for forward reach.

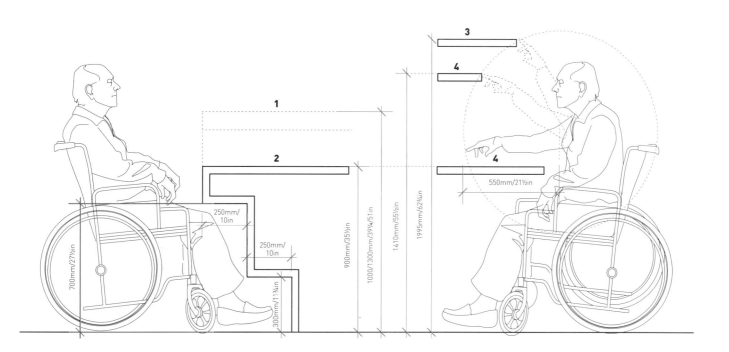

Balancing Priorities
Health Centre Reception Desk – Nomad

This reception desk has to satisfy the essentially conflicting aspirations to be welcoming and secure. It is therefore enclosed, almost a room, with the primary interface between staff and patients fortified by the glass screen that is also the principal decorative feature.

Below
Timber cladding connects wall to desk front to low curved wall to waiting area.

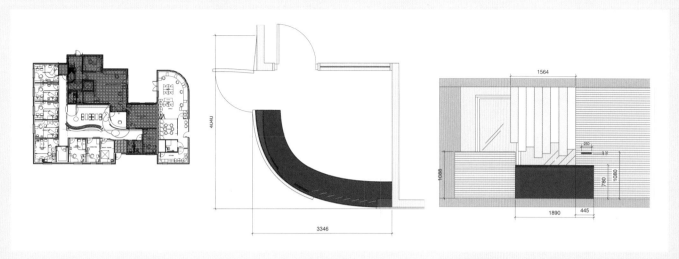

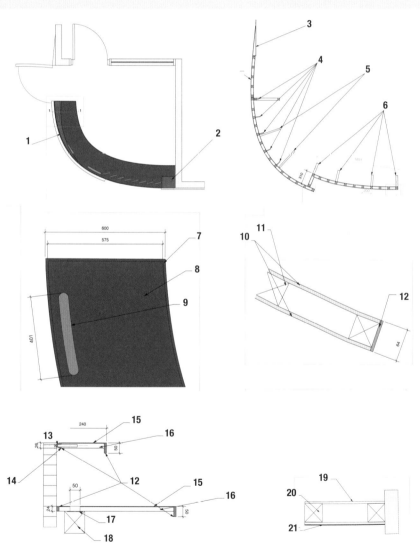

Above
Location plan, plan and elevation.

Left
1   High-level writing surface.
2   Repeat-prescription drop-off box.
3   Tapered section and access.
4   Häfele* concealed shaft support (high level), cat. no. 283.33.910.
5   495 x 330 x 30mm/19½ x 13 x 13in fixed bracket.
6   250 x 300 x 44mm/10 x 11¾ x 1¾in fixed bracket.
7   12.5mm/½in hardwood edging – painted Dulux 00NN07/000.
8   Forbo desktop Dessin 4168.
9   Cable grommet with rubber inlay.
10 7mm/¼in oak boards.
11 59 x 50mm/2¼ x 2in softwood framing.
12 Hardwood edge.
13 10mm-/½in-deep spacer painted to match hardwood edge – Dulux 00NN07/000.
14 Hafele concealed shelf support, cat. no. 283.33.910.
15 Forbo writing surface.
16 22mm/1in plywood.
17 Rubber teeth.
18 Cable-management basket.
19 6mm/¼in flexible MDF – painted Dulux 00NN07/000.
20 50 x 50mm/2 x 2in softwood frame.
21 Egger laminate U961 8T2 'Graphite'.

* Häfele, Dulux and Forbo are manufacturers and their names are included because their product is being exclusively specified for the project, to ensure both quality of performance and appearance.

The maximum number of persons working behind a desk at one time, which is determined by the traffic it must handle at peak times, will determine its functional length, but a front elevation may be stretched to increase its presence. A generous length of worktop also helps to keep the area behind the desk front, which is visible to visitors, tidier and so suggestive of organizational efficiency.

Right
Sections
1   High-level desk.
2   495 x 330 x 30mm/19½ x 13 x 1in fixed bracket.
3   250 x 300 x 44mm/10 x 11¾ x 1¾in fixed bracket.
4   Repeat-prescription drop-off box.
5   Recessed DDA area.
6   Access hatch.
7   Lock.
8   Metal gasket.
9   'Letter box' slot.
10 Secure lockable MDF box.

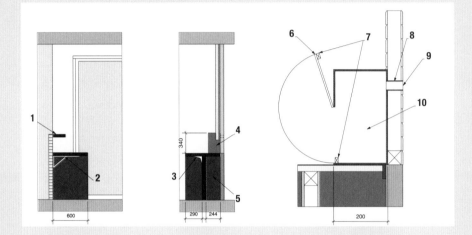

Right
Plan showing glass screen.

Middle
Plan of glass fins.

Far right
Setting out of fins.

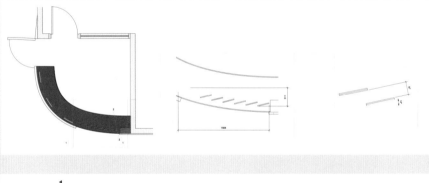

Right
Elevation of glass screen
1   Scholt 'Narima' toughened 10mm/½in laminated glass 4160 5.
2   Minimum and maximum heights above desk.

Far right above
Fixing detail for head of glass screen
5mm/¼in neoprene cover
1   50 x 50mm/2 x 2in softwood bracing. Bolt/ceiling plug to suit floor-plate construction.
2   Dorma Manet ceiling fixing.
3   10mm/½in laminated glass.
4   Suspended ceiling tiles.
5   Contractor to advise on site (a request that this detail is reconsidered when the extent and nature of the work is clear).
6   Silicone sealant.

Far right below
Plan of fixing at junction with ceiling tiles
1   Neoprene-wrapped softwood bracing.
2   Dorma Manet ceiling fixing.

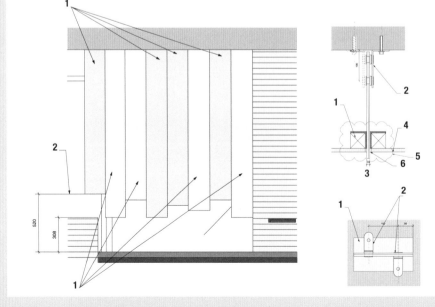

Above
The desk is made in sections for ease of transportation and access.

Left
Framing is prepared on site to receive hinges, locks and cables.

Analysing Function
University Library Reception Desk – Nomad

This reception desk for a university library is an example of how analysis of the particular role of a reception desk can generate form and features. It is conceived as a series of modular units that can be redeployed in other areas. The basic desk height is suitable for seated workers; when the boxes are set on top it becomes suitable for standing tasks. The projecting boxes provide a place for students to leave their baggage while engaged with staff and distinguish the checking-in section from the remainder of the multi-use desk.

Above
Projecting boxes, for student baggage, distinguish the checking-in section. The red strip, which contains cable distribution, becomes a decorative element and is turned down the side and matched by a slightly wider floor strip.

The drawings and dimensions, which are typical of those intended for a specialist contractor who will eventually make the piece, describe the form of the desk. The notes specify materials and clarify some ambiguous aspects of the drawing, such as the knee recess on the back elevation. While some suggestions, like the softwood box frame, are made for the construction method, these would be open for discussion between designer and contractor. The designer will be responsible for approving any proposals made by the contractor.

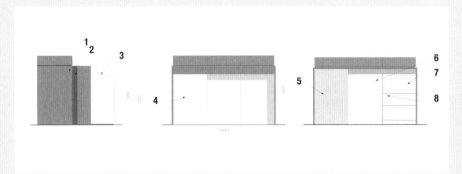

Elevations
1 3mm/¼in Wilson Art Solid Surface 9190-ML 'Black Star Melange'.
2 Formica insert – K2046 – 'Beaujolais'.
3 Ash-veneered box.
4 Front fascia and boxes to read as separate elements.
5 Knee recess.
6 Lockable cupboard unit.
7 Lockable drawer unit.
8 Ash veneer.

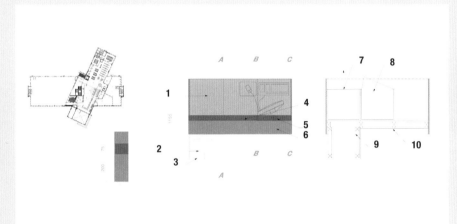

Plans
The left-hand plan shows the top and the right cuts through the storage level. The larger-scale detail on the left identifies a critical dimension.
1 Top boxes (see detail below).
2 Area for students' belongings.
3 Ash-veneered board.
4 Laminate insert.
5 Cable grommet.
6 Wilson Art Solid Surface 9190-ML 'Black Star Melange'.
7 3no. lockable drawers.
8 Lockable cupboard.
9 Softwood frame.
10 Ash-veneered panel.

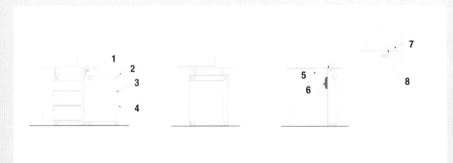

Sections (cut as indicated on the plans)
1 MDF panel painted Dulux 00NN07/000.
2 Mitred joints.
3 Softwood frame.
4 Ash-veneered cladding panel.
5 Recess for cable grommet.
6 Cable basket.
7 Cable trunking.
8 MDF grommet capping split into 2no. 250mm/10in sections faced with matching laminate.

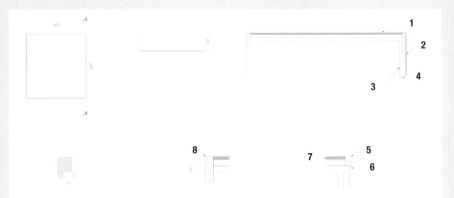

'Top box'
1 Forbo furniture linoleum 4186 'Charcoal'.
2 Open box faced with Wilson Art Solid Surface 9190-ML 'Black Star Melange'.
3 MDF painted Dulux 00NN07/000.
4 10mm/½in MDF painted Dulux 00NN07/000.
5 13mm/½in Wilson Art Edge 9190 ML 'Black Star Melange'.
6 Linoleum bonded to MDF board.
7 13mm/½in Wilson Art Edge 9190-ML 'Black Star Melange'.
8 3mm/¼in Wilson Art Solid Surface 9190-ML 'Black Star Melange' bonded to MDF board.

Other reception furniture

This tends to be specified rather than designed and, where space and budget permit, it normally consists of generous armchairs or sofas with, perhaps, a low-level table. It is in these areas that the corporate Modernist staples of Mies van der Rohe's and Lilly Reich's 'Barcelona' chair and Le Corbusier's and Charlotte Perriand's 'Grand Confort' are most likely to be encountered, with their suggestions of success and modernity. Reception areas are often also used as informal meeting areas; where possible, seating should be arranged to create separate areas in which two or three people can hold a semi-private conversation. Clusters of furniture can structure the disproportionately generous but often incoherent expanses of floor area devoted to reception activities at the entrance level of tall blocks.

Above
Seating can be as much about organizing and decorating the expanse of a reception area as it is about sitting.

Below
No one should have to wait long in reception so aesthetic impact can take precedence over creature comfort.

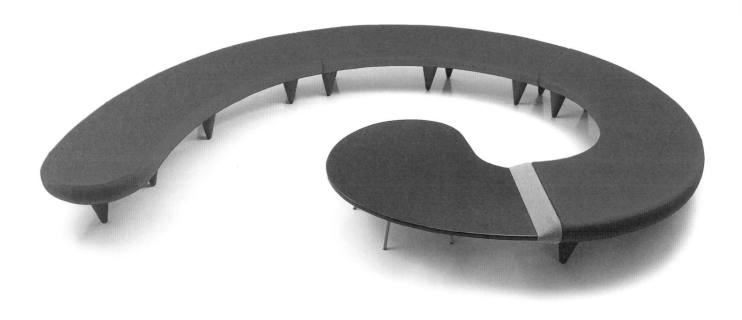

When organizations are large and multi-departmental the processing of visitors, which often involves their redirection to secondary reception spaces within the building, is labour-intensive. The reception desk often needs to accommodate several visitors at once and, for most organizations, the discretion offered by well-spaced individual reception points is desirable. Waiting times are, or can appear to be, protracted, particularly in public-service buildings. There is virtue in avoiding ranks of seating, all of which should ideally be in sight of reception staff so that visitors do not feel forgotten or ignored.

Above
Reception-area tables can divert visitors while they wait. The profusion, and confusion, of table legs, above, and the clarity of the X structure, in the centre, exercise the imagination.

Workspaces

There are many companies who specialize in the production of tables, chairs and storage equipment for office workspaces. Some produce mundane, cheap options, but a number, including the most successful, are constantly refining their products in response to what they see as emerging priorities for their customers. Their analyses and responses to perceived shifts have helped percolate innovation throughout the sector.

An office for one person requires a desk large enough to carry appropriate equipment and spread of papers. The office user, whether in a shared or individual office, requires a chair appropriate to his or her status. Chairs for visitors may be different since they are a place to hold a conversation for a comparatively brief time rather than for sustained work, but they should have a level of comfort on a par with but not exceeding that of the regular occupant. The quality of storage equipment has to complement that of the other pieces.

Workers in shared office spaces may work independently or collaboratively. Independents require a degree of visual separation, conventionally achieved by the provision of half-height screens. Collaborative workers share a large table or a grouping of individual tables, which form a hub for their shared activity. Some will work in both modes at different times and, for these, a degree of flexibility in the layout is necessary, achieved by separating grouped desks or adding desktop screens to subdivide surfaces. Tables that may be aggregated to form a unit and screens that may be added to subdivide areas form part of most specialist suppliers' ranges.

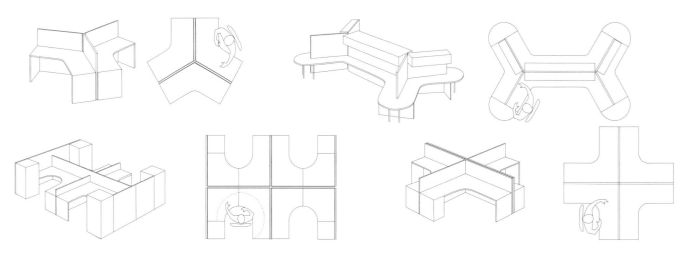

Above
Manufacturers produce coherent ranges that may be variously configured, with integrated elements for separation and storage.

Right
Much standard office furniture and many partition systems have limited aesthetic potential. Here coordination of furniture and mural enhance both.

In the public sector, offices are, generally, more modestly budgeted and more modestly scaled than those in the commercial sector, but rules about hierarchy and multiple occupancy are the same. The furniture will normally be specified and large public authorities often have approved suppliers whose limited ranges tend to be bland and therefore frustrating for ambitious designers. Fortunately, as in many other parts of the public sector, the lesson that good environments improve productivity and staff contentment is being learnt.

Some specialist manufacturers produce comprehensive ranges of equipment: some concentrate on individual pieces; some produce kits of parts, aesthetically consistent ranges of equipment that can be configured and reconfigured to suit precise activities.

Above
The cheapest partitioning units can still make effective work spaces. Expedient cable distribution and a well-worn floor surface contribute to this version of the emphatically relaxed aesthetic often favoured by creative organizations.

Left
Shared facilities are deemed to encourage informality and productive interaction.

Below
A speculation made in styrofoam and polyurea hot-spray, about mobility in the workplace. Office workers are no longer seen as permanently located at one desk position. Not all welcome this.

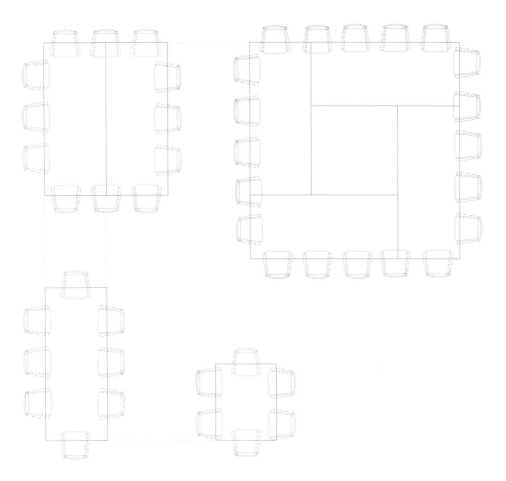

Left
Compatible tables can be adapted to suit work patterns.

Below
Furniture can define areas for small groups and individuals within open-plan, multi-levelled spaces.

Meeting rooms

Meeting rooms vary in size and number, relative to the size and method of operation of the business. A meeting room offers the opportunity, like the reception area, to express the ethos of the company, both to employees and the visitors who will use it. All participants in a meeting should feel equally entitled to express opinions. All should see and be seen equally. Usually a table is the focal point and controls how participants organize themselves. Chairs should be comfortable for at least an hour, and those for chairpersons may be a little grander to establish their status. It is not uncommon for large meeting rooms to be subdivided, and it is important to ensure when planning the room and choosing furniture for it that the two are compatible and that when the smaller rooms are merged the new dimensions and proportions allow the tables in both to be joined on their shorter ends to maximize the number of seating positions. It is also common for one or more secondary tables to be provided, usually positioned against a wall to carry documents and papers, or food and drink for distribution before or during a meeting.

The uses and sizes of meeting rooms vary with the principal activity of a public-sector institution, and furniture will normally be from an approved supplier. The need to allay suspicions of unnecessary extravagance will usually dictate a restrained solution.

Above
For some companies meeting spaces do not need visual and acoustic separation, only clear definition of territory.

Left
The proportions of a room should ensure that it works efficiently when subdivided.

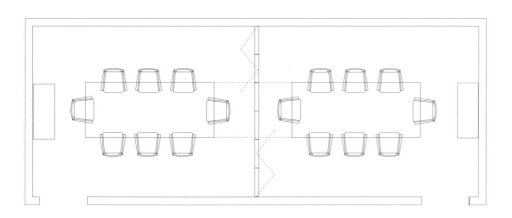

The presentation screen provides
a focus for the table in an
awkwardly shaped room created
by a curved external wall.

Boardrooms

A boardroom is a grander meeting room reserved for
the highest-ranking office holders in a private-sector
company. Their status should be reflected in the style
and standard of finish. However, since only the largest
and most traditionally structured companies are liable
to want such a thing, it may be appropriate to offer a
conservatively styled solution. The same considerations
about tables and chairs apply as in general meeting rooms,
but there may be more additional and elaborate pieces of
supplementary furniture, dispensing more extravagant
food and drink and displaying company memorabilia.

Hospitality

The 'hospitality sector' covers a wide spectrum of commercial activity. Quality of design is particularly important since there are few cafés, bars, restaurants or hotels that do not rely on the impact of their interiors to attract and retain customers. Furniture, specified and bespoke, is particularly important in the overall scheme of things given that chairs, tables and beds are defining elements in such spaces.

The commercial logic that demands a strong, clear identity and the number of identical project-specific pieces required mean that there is scope for batch production. While tables, particularly in the more expensive restaurants and hotels, are likely to be concealed by cloths, chairs and other seating pieces offer the most significant opportunities for establishing identity and providing visible justification for ambitious pricing. Often the nature, even the mechanics, of service offered, particularly in cafés, will change during the course of the day, and it is important to find an aesthetic that is convincing for all incarnations.

Hospitality-sector interiors and the furniture that contributes to their success is increasingly influenced by the escalation of changing fashions in what customers want to eat and drink and the contexts in which they consider it appropriate to do so. While appearance and atmosphere are the paramount aspirations, practical considerations of operation and materials must, as always, underpin decision-making.

All decisions are influenced by operational strategy. Cheaper outlets, like fast-food restaurants, rely on quick turnover of customers and easy maintenance, so finishes need to be hard and impervious, but it often takes very little to upgrade the most modest premises. The refrigerated glass-fronted display unit that is the interface between staff and customer in the smaller takeaway outlets can be transformed by the addition of a non-standard plinth.

Businesses with high profit margins want furniture that justifies their prices and encourages the customers who can afford them to stay longer and spend more. Cheaper outlets require less bulky furniture, to maximize seating places (or 'covers'), while expensive options will favour more generous dimensions both for individual pieces and table layouts, to provide greater privacy and space for more numerous and more attentive waiting staff. It is instructive and constructive for designers to make a rough calculation of the income a single seat can, with maximum occupancy, generate over a year. In this way it becomes easier to appreciate the anxiety of clients, particularly those with low profit margins, to maximize capacity.

Most customers will aspire to aural comfort and privacy, but as restaurants fill up and background noise levels rise, individuals will necessarily increase their own volume and so escalate the problem further. The equation between greater comfort and noise reduction is fortuitous in that it is in the more luxurious bars and restaurants that quiet, which speaks of exclusivity, is most desirable. The soft, absorbent pieces of furniture most frequently used in them can act as primary reduction agents. The more resonant, easy-to-clean, hard surfaces of cheaper options equally fortuitously contribute to the more vibrant

Far left
Furniture can consolidate identity. The white stools slump like ice cream in a cone.

Left
A standard, glass-fronted refrigerated cabinet is set behind a white acrylic shelf, which doubles as a counter top, and a wooden display shelf.

environments to which their target customers are likely to aspire.

All areas within the sector offer opportunities for bespoke furniture design particular not only to generic categories but to individual projects. All should take shape after consultation with the client, first to assess priorities and then to consider improvements in established practice, to identify a pragmatic solution that will ensure efficient operation before any conceptual commitment is made. Reception desks in hotel lobbies and restaurants will house computers, telephones and the mechanics of payment. These and other mundane pieces of equipment are generally screened from public view. Restaurants frequently have 'waiter stations', for cutlery and napery, in customers' vision, and these utilitarian objects should contribute to a collective aesthetic. All offer opportunities for bespoke solutions.

Reception desks in hotels share many of the practical requirements of reception desks for offices. However, rather than being devoted to greeting and redirecting guests they also need to cope with procedures of checking in, settling bills and giving information. The equipment required is no more complex than that for office reception desks but, since the interaction between staff and guests is longer, clear separation between workstations is desirable. In contrast to office receptionists who sit, hotel tradition seems to demand that staff stand, perhaps as a hangover from times when room keys were hung on a board behind them and required a few steps to access.

The provision of separate desks, each for one staff member, is becoming more common. Another change which is becoming more common is, inevitably, online checking in and, in the spirit of digital informality this is often provided for with flat-screen computer terminals on a table, usually high enough for guests to use while standing, with high stools as a concession to comfort.

Reception areas can be small or they can be large and double as lounges. In the latter case they will have sofas and armchairs, usually arranged in social groupings. Such places will normally flow past minimal dividing structures into bars and restaurants. Increasingly, they will provide internet access, including WiFi.

Opposite and below
Nhow Hotel reception and servery.
A reception desk is usually the
first expression of a project's
aesthetic and will set the theme for
variations throughout the whole.

Right
The sand and cement render on
the face and top of this hotel
reception desk makes a transition
between the rough textures
and patterns of a concrete wall
retained from the original building
shell, the precision of the new
window and door openings, and
the bridge parapet at mezzanine
level. A wooden section provides
a more sympathetic surface for
the necessary transactions.

Hotel Lobby Subdivision
Feasibility Study – Ab Rogers Design

Hotel lobbies are usually multi-functional, containing areas for reception, waiting and recreation, bars, cafés and restaurants. They may also be divided into territories for residents and non-residents. While in traditional hotels each activity might have a dedicated room, it is now customary to remove walls to make grander spaces and to allow, and encourage, freer movement between areas.

Where spaces flow one into the other, different furniture pieces and layouts demarcate dedicated areas but frequently something more significant may be desirable without the opaque bulk of a solid wall. The screens illustrated in this study were developed for a chain of mid-range hotels and, in addition to subdividing zones, support images of local landmarks and televisions for entertainment and information.

In both examples fixings must be made at floor and ceiling levels. High-level fixings must be made to structural pieces which may require continuing the uprights through a suspended ceiling plane and the provision of a cover piece or collar at those points to allow movement and mask local irregularities in finishes. The attached banquette seating in the second example increases stability at base level.

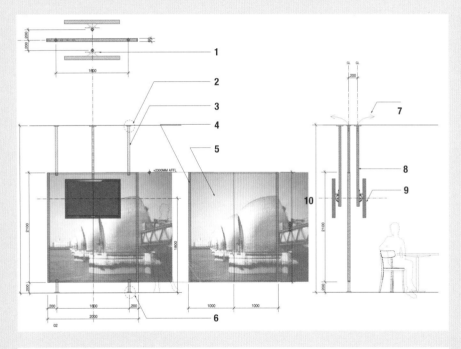

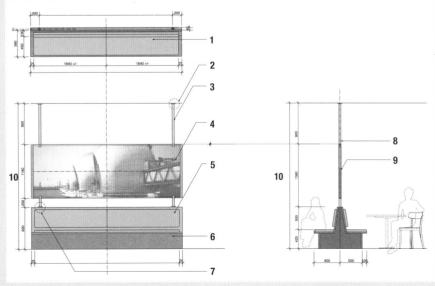

Space divider with television
1. TV bracket fixed to ceiling.
2. Flange screwed to ceiling structure.
3. Powder-coated steel frame.
4. Powder-coated steel U-frame to support acrylic panels.
5. Panels with laminated images.
6. Foot screwed to structural floor.
7. Cabling feed through metal frame into ceiling void.
8. TV bracket fixed to ceiling.
9. TV hung on ceiling bracket.
10. Internal ceiling height.

Space divider with banquette seating
1. 50mm/2in upholstered foam cushion fixed with Velcro strips.
2. Flange screwed to ceiling structure.
3. Powder-coated steel frame.
4. Acrylic panels with laminated images.
5. 50mm/2in upholstered foam cushion fixed with Velcro strips.
6. MDF seating carcass.
7. Foot screwed to seating carcass.
8. Powder-coated steel frame.
9. Powder-coated steel U to support acrylic panels.
10. Internal ceiling height.

Hotel bedrooms

Bedroom furniture lends itself to batch production. The advent of the 'boutique' hotel established a new aesthetic and ambition for both expensive and middle-range hotels, and this has filtered down through strata of tariffs so that only the most isolated, cash-strapped businesses have since failed to engage with it. The basic provision of components has remained much the same. Space for hanging clothes remains a fundamental requirement and no successful alternative to the wardrobe has emerged, although the basic cupboard is frequently customized to provide suitcase storage, as well as space for an ironing board, minibar, kettle and sometimes a safe. The system of grading hotel bedrooms, which influences and justifies prices, specifies the level of equipment required for qualification at each level. This inevitably encourages ambitious over-packing of prescribed items into rooms hard-stretched to accommodate them, which requires intelligent specification. While solid, plump upholstery may signal luxury, lighter pieces on spindly legs signal modernity and expose more floor area, which in turn implies space.

The bed structure itself is seldom of consequence since it will normally be concealed beneath rhetorical layers of bedding, suggesting luxurious generosity, but the bedhead remains crucial as a way of establishing some distinctive identity for the hotel as a whole and for the more practical chore of carrying reading lights and the switches that control an increasing battery of additional light fittings and electrical devices. It is important to consider how a reading light used by one occupant of the room will affect the sleep of the other. Bedroom chairs and tables tend to be specified. There are manufacturers who specialize in hotel

Above
Restrained furniture makes no attempt to compete with the existing cornice and painted ceiling.

Left
Bedroom furniture can be comparatively modest, secondary in this opulent suite to the glass-walled wet room.

furniture but their products tend to be conservative, and it is more rewarding to look beyond their catalogues.

In new-build projects, bathrooms are increasingly dealt with as prefabricated, pre-plumbed and pre-fitted 'pods' that are lowered into the skeletal structural frame before internal partitions are built. Fittings and finishes are normally specified rather than designed and made. In conversion work, particularly with generous budgets, the aspiration to introduce individuality and the idiosyncrasies of existing spaces make more opportunities for free-standing and built-in bespoke pieces.

The way hotel rooms are used has seen significant changes, inevitably in response to the emergence of digital technologies but also to broader shifts in behaviour. The 'dressing table' has become increasingly redundant, as it has in homes. Its drawers are seldom used by short-term occupants, who make up the majority of customers in non-resort hotels, and its triptych of mirrors has been supplanted by provisions within the luxurious bathrooms to which grooming has migrated. Table provision has been discreetly wired for digital connection but this is already becoming redundant and expedient surface-mounted wiring has been superseded by WiFi provision. The travelling businessperson is likely to spend the equivalent of a working day in the bedroom and prefers a table that is more reminiscent of an office desk and a chair with something of the mobility and adaptability of the office chair in place of the lumpen armchair.

For most newly built budget hotels there is a financial imperative to maximize the number of bedrooms, thus minimizing bedroom floor area. Until recently the standard plan has been a bath/shower room to the right or left of the entrance door with clothes and luggage storage opposite it and the bed occupying the centre of the remaining floor area with a dressing table, television, chair and small table for room service squeezed into the remaining perimeter space. Furniture was blandly inoffensive whether bought from a specialist supplier or bespoke.

Below
The bed, along with other practical necessities, makes a composite unit that sits distinctly apart from the elements of the original room.

Below right
The dimensions and configuration of a bed need not, probably should not, change but the bedhead can offer an opportunity for detailed decoration.

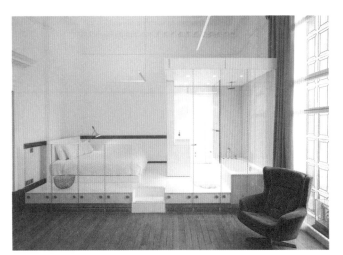

Bedroom Options
Feasibility Study – Ab Rogers Design

These four plans illustrate optional room layouts, for a budget hotel chain, in which the conventional four-square mass of the shower room is remodelled within an overall layout that recognizes more informal lifestyles, the fact that people shower rather than bath, and the need to provide a dedicated workplace. All break away from the usual, overly familiar rectilinear planning.

Plan A
The bath/shower room block is angled and curved, the furniture for clothes hanging, hot drink preparation and work are built into the structure. The bed squarely confronts the wall-mounted television.

Plan B
The bed is integrated into the bath/shower room. The desk completes the potentially complex and intricate amalgam of wall and furniture.

Plan C
A variation on B that allows easier access to the bed for a second occupant.

Plan D
The most radical reworking of the bath/shower box.

1   Entrance.
2   Shower room.
3   Clothes hanging.
4   Hot drink preparation.
5   Desk.
6   Bed.
7   Luggage under.
8   Television.

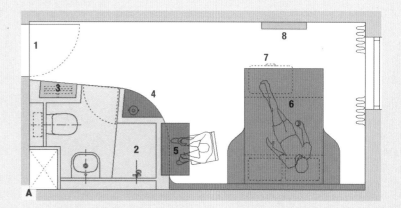

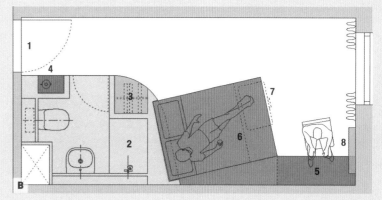

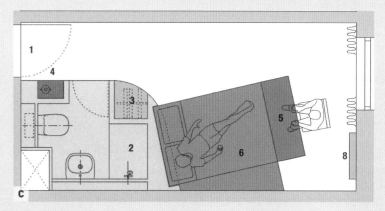

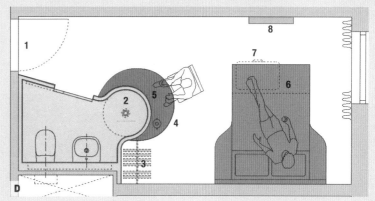

Bars and restaurants

The word 'bar' first referred to the original and continuing role of the counter over which food and drink were dispensed as a barrier that prevents customers from accessing staff territory but its definition has evolved to identify the room in which the counter is placed and has become the generic term for the spectrum of drinking places, from the robust 'public' bar through the more genteel 'lounge' to the fragile elegance of the 'cocktail' bar. Changes in social habits have broadened the range of activities and bar counters increasingly carry and conceal specialist equipment for dispensing drinks and serving food.

In cafés and bars, refrigerators, sinks and shelves are packed behind the decorative screen of the service-counter front. It is common for a range of displayed drinks, refrigerators and shelving on the wall behind the service zone to augment the provision behind the counter. The presentation of bottles on the 'back bar' becomes more critical than that of items tucked under the counter worktop. Refrigerators, which are produced by specialist manufacturers, will be specified but will justify the extra money spent on their appearance. Detailing of shelves may use proprietary products but these leave significant opportunity for ingenuity. The 'gantry', the high-level storage of clean glasses above the front bar, offers an opportunity for site- and project-specific design. The space between back bar and front counter should be no more than 900mm, enough to let staff pass each other comfortably but close enough for easy movement between front and back.

A well-ordered and decorated back bar.

Above
Untidy elements including games machines are collected below a new projecting bulkhead.

Left
Fixed furniture pieces create a variety of defined territories within a monumental volume.

The location of the bar counter may be determined as much by access to plumbing and other services as by aesthetic priorities. It deals with the core business of ordering, serving and paying, and the back-up practicalities of washing and drying glasses. Crockery and cutlery will normally be dealt with, out of sight, in the kitchen area. The work surface for washing glasses and mixing drinks is normally at the conventional worktop height of approximately 900mm/35½in with a depth of 600mm/23½in but is partly shielded from customers' view by a front shelf, which is raised to between 1050mm/41¼in and 1150mm/45¼in above floor level and is typically between 250mm/9¾in and 400mm/16¾in wide, enough to support customers' glasses without inhibiting service. Customers choosing to sit at the counter will perch on high stools, usually between 650mm/25½in and 800mm/31½in high, with a footrest to help balance. A rail attached to the counter front will provide foot support and some protection for the lower face of the counter. In bars that have waiting staff servicing tables, an area of counter will usually be designated for their exclusive use so that they do not have to compete with customers for attention and their preferential treatment is not resented. In bars where all orders are taken and served by waiting staff, the counter may be comparatively small with no provision for customer seating.

High stools at the bar are traditionally the resort of the solitary drinker and have acquired a degree of glamour, suggesting a more intimate, perhaps therapeutic, relationship with staff. Even where the stools are seldom

The right choice of furniture can complement lighting effects. Here white chairs and tables are tinted by the dominant ambient colour and their curves relate to the wall and reflected floor patterns.

used they contribute to the mythology of bar culture. They can also contribute to identity in non-alcoholic catering environments, such as coffee bars and fast-food restaurants, where they can evoke another kind of nostalgia for other glamorized eras and cultures.

Seating and tables in the remainder of the bar are normally at conventional heights, particularly where food is served formally. Where customers only drink or eat snack foods, lower seating, such as sofas and armchairs, and correspondingly low tables are acceptable.

There is in every bar, café or restaurant a 'best' table, which is in the most desirable location and usually exists in its own clearly articulated space. It can be different for different businesses and customer types but generally it will be located next to a significant physical element, a wall or a column, something that implies special status, and a degree of enclosure. The least successful tables are those that sit in the middle of an unarticulated expanse of floor and the solution is to break down this amorphous area into a number of discrete places. Non-structural elements, walls and columns, may be introduced but, where these break up the space to an unacceptable degree, banquettes and booths, made psychologically secure by backs that are high enough to imply privacy, create as many desirable locations as can be squeezed into the plan. Where subdivision is not an option a solution is to put bigger, preferably round, tables in the middle of the space. Larger groups feel more secure than small and a round table makes for a self-contained experience as the group form a circle in which each can see all others.

Above
'Hooded' chairs give enclosure and a sense of privacy and punctuate the length of the continuous wall bench.

Left
Fixed furniture pieces create a variety of defined areas within a monumental volume.

A Strategic Approach
Bar Ten – Ben Kelly Design

A café, a bar or a restaurant that has an established clientele need not indulge in high concept transformations and might, in fact, do better to preserve whatever qualities it possesses, however intangible. A new business or one with competition needs to assert its character.

Taking its cue from its gritty location and the heavy existing columns that dominated its empty shell, this bar is characterized by ostentatiously over-engineered detailing. Hard finishes, terrazzo, steel and raw plaster dominate, and unupholstered wooden stools and bench seating become, by default, the concession to comfort.

Left
The dark green terrazzo floor tiles also clad the bar front and the wall behind. The steel stool supports rise from cast, raised, terrazzo feet.

Bottom left
The granite bar shelf hovers above the solid tiled bar front on stainless-steel brackets.

Bottom right
Heavy steelwork supports the seat and backrest of the banquette seating.

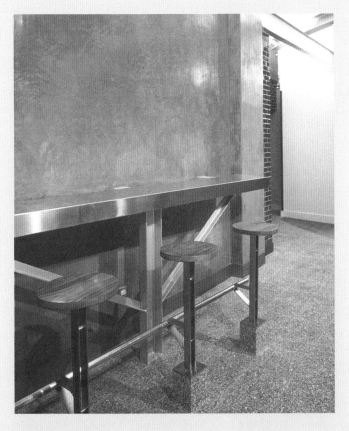

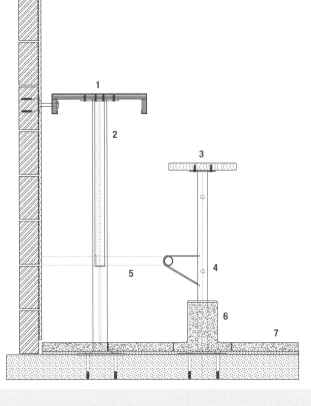

Above
The stainless-steel wall shelf is supported
on substantial steel sections and the footrest
on the stools' paired steel stems.

Above right
Section.

Below
Elevation.
1   Stainless-steel shelf/table.
2   Steel structure.
3   Wooden seat.
4   Paired stainless steel
    supports bolted to terrazzo base.
5   Stainless-steel foot rail.
6   Terrazzo base.
7   Terrazzo floor tiles.

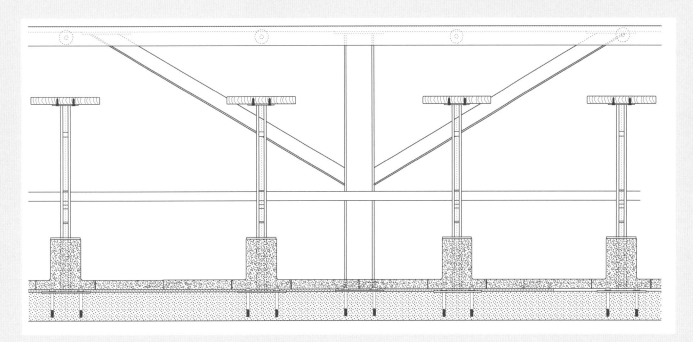

There is no obligation to adapt bar counters for disabled users while there is alternative provision at tables and room to manoeuvre wheelchairs into position. However, just as the mandatory obligation has reshaped the block of reception desks, there is a possibility of reconsidering the profile of the bar counter to create a length at conventional table heights, free of sinks and without the front upstand, that can be used to serve and consume.

Traditionally bars are primarily nocturnal environments; hence, good lighting design is crucial in creating atmosphere. Manufacturers and suppliers will normally provide free advice about performance and installation but will only offer equipment from their own ranges. Independent consultants will charge a fee but will consider all available options and should be employed where an ambitious lighting solution is anticipated. Given the technical complications of designing electrical equipment, and the risks and responsibilities involved in doing so, for most jobs it is logical to choose from the options presented in manufacturers' catalogues. Technical risks are eliminated and responsibility transferred if proprietary light sources are fitted in accordance with their makers' instructions. Fittings may be surface-mounted or concealed behind translucent materials. Wall benches, booths and banquettes offer opportunities for concealed light sources. Light may spill through apertures to wash visible surfaces. Fluorescent and LED fittings are commonly used as concealed sources.

Above and above left
A more robust aesthetic demands a much more intense light behind red translucent acrylic inserts.

Left
A light source behind the downstand of the bar counter emphasizes the incised lines on the bar front.

Left
A gentler light is enough to throw the layered tiles on the bar front, which are matched by those on the wall, into relief.

Below
Backlit translucent acrylic panels in a plywood counter front.

Below
Lighting and wiring. The
modelling of bar fronts, to
provide knee and toe spaces for
customers and staff leave room for
electrical wiring and light fittings.

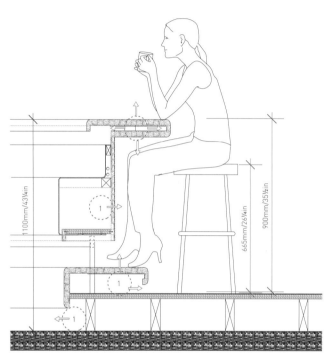

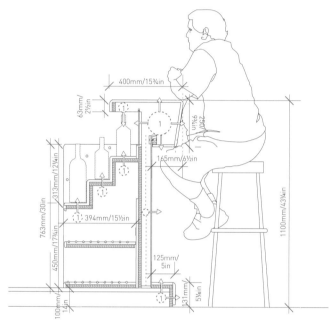

Storage, above and behind bar counters, of glasses and bottles of clear or translucent liquids provides surfaces that exploit artificial lighting. Operating convenience has led to a battery of bottles and dispensers ranged on the wall behind the bar counter, often set in front of a mirror, and to the 'gantry', high-level storage shelves or racks for clean glasses above the counter. Gantries are necessarily low to allow easy access for bar staff, and the impact of reflected and refracted light through polished glass is the greater because of that.

Specialist companies manufacture equipment used in the preparation and serving of food and drink and will normally provide planning services and carry out the installation. The collating of information about the size and most effective sequencing of equipment, refrigerators, sinks, glass-washing machines, tills, credit-card terminals and the like, is fundamental to successful counter design.

Specialist manufacturers will also provide advice about heating and air-conditioning installations. These are normally mounted at ceiling level and the ductwork is concealed behind suspended ceilings.

While this free consultancy service will be adequate for most projects, it becomes the designer's responsibility to lessen, or eliminate, the visual impact of necessary pieces of equipment. Heating and lighting sources can be incorporated within and behind ranges of built-in seating.

Bar counters have to withstand heavy customer use, frequent cleaning and the corrosive effects of spilt food and drink. In kitchens and stores, practicality can supersede the aesthetic priorities of public areas and stainless steel is the most common material for storage, worktops and splashbacks. In public areas, appearance is more crucial. Hardwood, the traditional material, wears well and acquires a patina that speaks of traditional qualities. In a fashion-conscious market not many businesses are now willing to sustain evidence of the first raw degradation in the transition from the pristine freshness of natural materials to well-worn character. Glass, metals or man-made composites, such as solid-colour core acrylics, are better able to resist ageing.

Top

This island bar is organized
to make two self-contained
and mirrored workstations.
The Hallion bar top layout
Work surface layout

1 Wine and spirits.
2 Preparation surface.
3 Ice sink with three divisions.
4 Prep sink.
5 Draught beer.
6 Hand-wash basin.
7 Two-door chiller below.
8 Three-door chiller below.

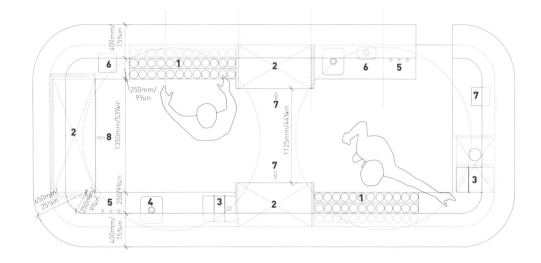

Middle

The Hallion bar sub worktop layout
1 Sub-work surface layout.
2 Two-door chiller.
3 Three-door chiller.
4 Till.
5 Prep sink.
6 Ice sink.
7 Hand-wash basin.
8 Front-loading bin.
9 Draught beer taps.
10 Top-loading bottle bin.

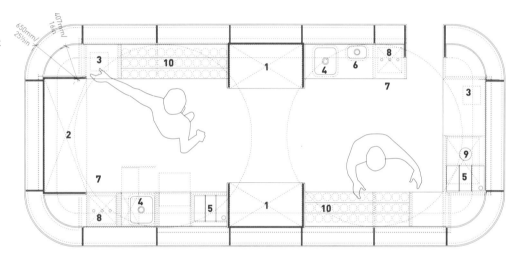

Bottom

The floor within the bar area
is raised to accommodate
service pipes – and to give
height and authority to staff.

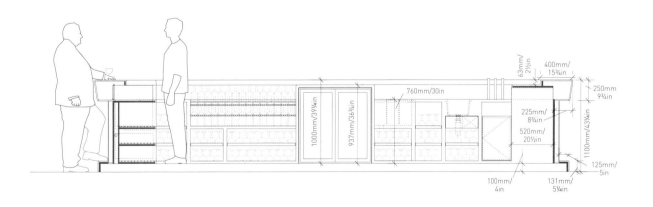

Fine-Tuning
Merus Winery – UXUS Design

This is not quite a bar. It offers something other than a place for social interaction. It sets out to be convivial but is primarily concerned with persuading visitors to buy in bulk from the vineyard, of which it is the public face. Like many such enterprises, it draws on the iconography of wine, the mechanics of its storage and the luxury of its consumption, but it works more ambitious variations on the themes than most, recognizing that its clientele is unlikely to be seduced by kitsch. It exemplifies how identification and concentration on the essence of a brief can fine-tune the predictable.

Top
Prefabricated concrete storage 'bins' line the walls and replicate the stone storage elements in traditional wine cellars.

Bottom
Black-stained, turned timber plinths, on which to rest glasses and bottles, are reminiscent of chess pieces and suggest high-minded hedonism.

Left
The cliché of wine barrel ends fixed to the wall is relieved by their being painted to match it.

Below left
The well-tried tactic of a miscellaneous chair collection is employed but elevated by the quality of the pieces chosen. The lacquered tabletop behaves like a mirror.

Below
The irregular stacking of this storage unit, its horizontality prompted by the practical necessity of storing bottles on their side and an impulse to avoid the predictable patterns of conventional shelving, retains some of the informality of the cellar bar. Natural timber grain and colour are accentuated by the black staining of the other elements.

Fixed seating and tables

There are two kinds of fixed seating. The simplest, the bench or banquette, is a continuous run along the length of a wall and is commonly used in restaurants, bars and cafés. Combined with unfixed tables and chairs, it uses a comparatively modest floor area and usefully provides flexibility of layout. Tables for two, with one customer sitting on the wall 'bench', may be organized separately and, when required, may be grouped to accommodate larger numbers.

Booths – self-contained fixed seating and tables – are most commonly found in restaurants or the more expensive bars. When compared to conventional arrangements of loose chairs and tables, they consume a disproportionate amount of floor space. While they may be constructed against a wall, they are most strategically useful when located in the middle of amorphous spaces to structure subdivision and give each table a well-defined and semi-private location.

Left
The basic form of the dining booth can be evolved into something extraordinary.

Below
Fixed elements make secure and intimate spaces.

Above

The continuous undulating sweep of backrest clearly defines an area within the bigger space.

Left

A less exotic construction in an office building: timber boards on high metal frames consolidate individual booths. A suspended banner encloses the third side.

Two tiers of booths bring drama and maximize seating capacity.

A continuous wall bench takes structural support from the wall and only requires regular support for the seat and backrest. Typically it is upholstered on the back and seat, but upholstery may also extend down the front vertical face, reducing the need for refined finishing of the basic structure. Often the back cushion will be high enough to act as a headrest, or higher; this expanse of soft material will also enhance the acoustic performance of the room. Cushions are frequently fixed with Velcro tape to facilitate removal for cleaning. Carcassing, the concealed framing structure, can be made from any sheet material but plywood or MDF are the most popular, the former when a natural timber finish is required and the latter for a paint finish. Sheet materials may be cut in a specialist workshop to make a series of identical rib profiles, which will support the horizontal and vertical planes of seat and backrest, eliminating the need for complex on-site framed construction. Seat and back elements need be no more than five degrees off the vertical and horizontal, but such angles are crucial for comfort.

Upholstery usually takes the form of long cushions, with their junctions responding to the setting out of table positions. If seating runs between two flanking walls there is no need for special end detailing to the substructure, but where an end is exposed the extruded section must be brought to a satisfactory visual conclusion. There are options: an end panel, which may perform as an armrest

or be as high as the backrest, will be adequate to cover cut ends and contain the cushions, or the sheets that make up the substructure of seat and back may project beyond the upholstered sections to signify an ending.

Spaces between tables in front of a wall bench can be, and often are, tight because of the economic pressure to maximize customer numbers. The unfixed table can be moved by waiting staff, or customers, to provide more generous access. In densely packed fast-food restaurants, tables are often fixed to the floor to maintain the integrity of the seating layout in the face of heavy use, but space between them is usually tight enough to allow easy communication between adjacent tables.

Booths

Booths take up a significant amount of floor area per seat and this, together with the relatively high cost of construction, means that they tend to be used in more expensive bars and restaurants. Ease of access is the defining consideration in their design, particularly when the long axis of a table is at right angles to a wall. Tables and seats are normally fixed and usually each unit will seat two or four people. The configuration often demands some wriggling on the part of customers taking the inner positions and collaboration with those on the outside when they wish to leave. The fixed elements present some minor problems for waiting staff, who have to serve across customers sitting on the outside. Where there is sufficient circulation space, an additional loose chair may be placed at the end of the table. Banquettes with a circular plan provide inward-looking privacy but they consume even greater amounts of floor space, much of it lost between the abutting quadrants. A footprint of between 200 and 220 degrees will suggest enclosure without inhibiting access too severely.

Booths are generally difficult for disabled access and, for wheelchair users, only feasible if the wheelchair can be positioned at the end of the table, without blocking a circulation route.

The separating elements between booths, which are effectively walls, may be high or low as appropriate. The higher they are, particularly in the centre of rooms, the more privacy they offer. Where booths are grouped the backs may butt together, but the need to assimilate structural components tends to result in a thickness of at least 100mm/4in. This can become a useful base on which to fix standard light-fittings or racks for customer clothes and baggage in the French bistro tradition. The voids created under and between adjacent booths

and walls may also be useful for the circulation of air-conditioning equipment, and the horizontal strips between them is a location for input and extract grills.

Light sources to wash across walls and floors are easily located behind or under built-in furniture. The most frequent solution is to incorporate strip lighting, usually with a translucent diffuser to reduce glare, in the space between the back of seating units and the wall. This creates an even gradation of tone, brightest nearest the source. Light sources to wash across floors can be located in skirting-level recesses and it is normal to ensure that they are adequately protected against damage from shoes. For all locations, spotlights in place of strip lights will create a pattern in which sharp-edged areas of brightness at the source bleed off in parabolas of decreasing intensity. A raised floor within the booth increases the sense of its being a special place, even if it complicates further the practicalities of accessibility.

There is the possibility of combining wall bench or banquette and booth, in which the long axis of the table runs parallel to the circulation zone. This offers marginally more flexibility and marginally easier access for customers and serving staff. In this configuration, two or more customers may sit at the wall and two on the ends of the table, all on fixed seating, with an option for loose chairs at the front of the table, which is often moveable to ease access.

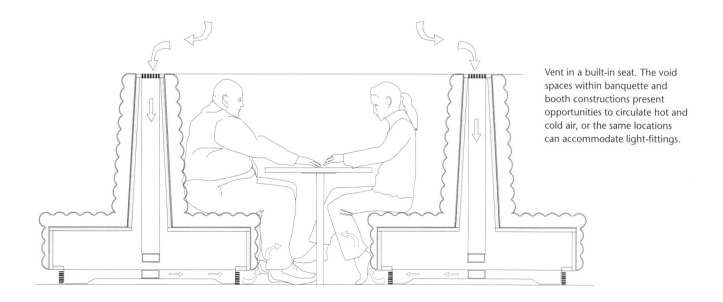

Vent in a built-in seat. The void spaces within banquette and booth constructions present opportunities to circulate hot and cold air, or the same locations can accommodate light-fittings.

Exhibition design

The lifespan of an exhibition might be no more than a day; on the other hand, it might be permanent. In either incarnation it will involve the creation of pieces of furniture of varying degrees of sophistication. It will not necessarily be the case that furniture for exhibitions of short duration should be expediently made from cheap materials. Brief exhibits can be prestigious and furniture should complement content. All exhibitions should look as though they have been taken seriously, without necessarily looking serious.

Whether furniture is intended as a permanent component in a museum's resources or a temporary exhibition the criteria are the same. The objects on display must be easily seen, from the most informative and flattering perspective, sometimes in the round, which will mean a freestanding cabinet. Sometimes a single viewpoint, in a wall-mounted cabinet, will do. Sometimes a single object will warrant its own display, sometimes

a number will be collected together in a cabinet, either because they contribute to the same story or do not justify singular treatment.

Visitors are often in close contact with exhibition furniture as they scrutinize objects. Cabinets and other display items need to support the weight of visitors leaning on them. Without diverting attention from the exhibits, they must stand up to scrutiny because exhibition structures, no matter how modest their budgets, must complement their content.

There are, however, exceptions to the principle that exhibitions should play a secondary role to the material they display. When subject matter is not primarily visual, as in informative and interpretative exhibitions where factual material is usually supported by a high graphic content and there is a necessary predominance of text, exhibition furniture must provide identity. In trade shows, which are essentially competitive exhibitions in which companies or institutions take part in sales and promotion contests, spectacle is important. Organizers of trade shows rely on a large number of exhibitors from within a defined sector to offer visitors a broad enough range of products to maximize attendance. The events are typically held within cavernous and characterless sheds and the assertion of exhibitors' presence and identity are at least as important as the display of products, which may be as visually unprepossessing as financial services and engineering

Below
In museums, visibility and security are the two primary, and potentially conflicting, requirements. Consultation with the manufacturers of security systems is crucial from the beginning of the design process.

Below right
A temporary exhibition structure should have authority and an assertive presence when competing for attention with other exhibits.

grommets. The relative flamboyance of exhibition furniture should perhaps be in inverse proportion to that of the exhibition content. Often with unappealing visual content the enticement of seating, perhaps drinks and modest food, will be used as a lure for visitors weary from tramping around an excess of exhibits. Opportunities exist for bespoke pieces but often the limited time available for installation favours bought furniture – which may be reused – or furniture hired for the duration of the exhibition. In such commercial environments where it is in organizers' interests to maximize the number of events they offer, time spent assembling an exhibition on site is limited, so elements are prefabricated and installed by specialist companies some of which will offer a design service. When an independent designer is commissioned it is normal, and good practice, to select and collaborate with the fabricator from an early stage in the process.

Security is a crucial consideration for all exhibitions. For some, usually those with demonstrably valuable contents, the need will be self-evident and requirements will be specified by owners, lenders or insurance companies. They may also specify levels of environmental control. For exhibitions with less obviously vulnerable content, the factors influencing security strategies are variable. They depend on the level of invigilation and the portability of the objects. Cheap and modest objects may tempt thieves just because they are on show. Layout will be important if invigilators are to have uninterrupted views of all areas. Access to cabinets and cases is important for permanent or long-term exhibitions. For short-term ones, lids and doors may be screwed in place, which is cheaper than providing lockable access. Acrylic is more easily dealt with than glass. Much display furniture need not be robust.

Both the content and the anticipated audience for an exhibition should influence design. Since visitors are likely to be sympathetic to the content of an exhibition they choose to attend, furniture style should complement that of the exhibits. As in retail design, furniture should not overwhelm the objects it presents but may need to support or flatter modest but important pieces. Again as in retail design, much of the making will be done off site and access routes for large pieces should be checked.

Collaboration with specialist exhibition fabricators and installers, who are almost invariably the same company, holds good for all types of exhibitions. While museums may be prepared to allow, and sometimes seem to expect, more time for installation work the museum environment is not suitable for elaborate production work, which is more effectively carried out in specialist workshops.

Whatever an exhibition's location and configuration, consideration must be given, from the beginning of the design process, to lighting and security and the wiring for both, and both again warrant the support of specialist consultants.

Designers normally give fabricators drawings, specifying dimensions and materials, and decisions about the most effective way of realizing these are developed in conversation between both parties. It is another instance where lead decisions about appearance are most effectively made by the designer and those about production most productively made by the specialist contractor who will also be focused on the problems of transportation and assembly.

Below
A modest structure will acquire presence if made exclusively from an equally modest material.

A Permanent Exhibition
Postal Museum – Nick Coombe Architecture

Increasingly, museums are using sound to convey, and increase the amount of, information that would once have been restricted to printed captions. This inevitably prompts pieces of furniture dedicated to audiovisual display provision. In this example, the same basic configuration is adapted to suit three locations.

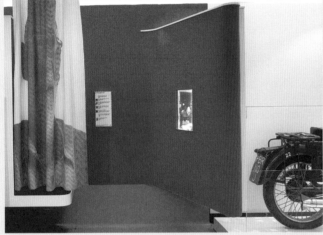 

Above left
Audio booth 2.

Below
The image screen in booth 3 is on the right.

Above right
The curtain, with the screenprinted image, to audio booth 1 is on the left.

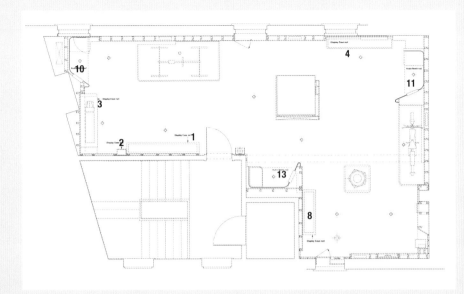

Left

1 Display case 1.
2 Display case 2.
3 Display case 3.
4 Display case 4.
5 Display case 5.
6 Display case 6.
7 Display case 7.
8 Display case 8.
9 Display case 9.
10 Audio booth 1.
11 Audio booth 2.
12 Audio booth 3.
13 Film monitor.
14 Entrance.
15 Fire-extinguisher housing.
16 Radiators concealed by graphics panel.
17 Window.
18 Exhibit display base.
19 Equipment.
20 Visitor interactive.

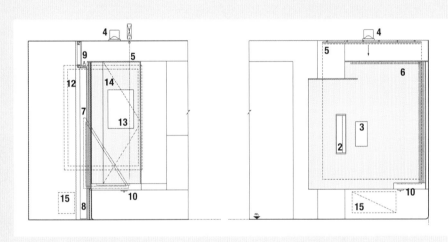

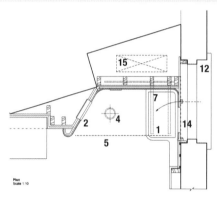

Plan
Scale 1:10

Above
Audio booth 1
1 Seat with rubber surface.
2 Backlit image panel.
3 Information panel.
4 Ceiling speaker.
5 Curtain with screenprinted image.
6 Orange carpet facing.
7 Mild-steel structure.
8 Softwood structure to secondary wall.
9 Fluorescent uplighting trough.
10 Rotary sound volume under seat.
11 Vinyl floor material taken up coving to face wall.
12 Window.
13 Aperture in panel.
14 Opening panel to access window for cleaning.
15 Equipment.

Left
Display case 8mm/¼in toughened laminated glass.
1 Spray-painted 18mm/¾in MDF
    facing on softwood carcass.
2 2mm/⅛in powder-coated mild-steel glazing frame.
3 Exhibit mount.
4 Spray-painted 18mm/¾in MDF panel
    with screen-painted graphics.
5 Vinyl floor taken over coving and up wall.
6 Mild-steel powder-coated caption plates.

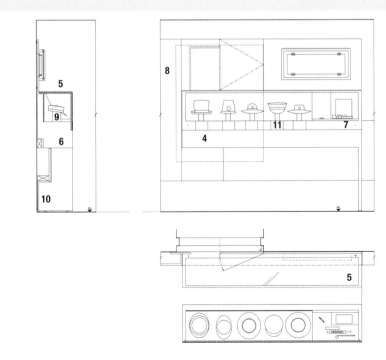

A Temporary Exhibition
British Design 1948–2012 – Ben Kelly Design

The scale of structures for this six-month exhibition both grouped miscellaneous artefacts and subdivided the existing gallery. Angled walls ensured stability without the need to make any significant connections to existing walls.

Above
A double-sided freestanding exhibition structure with plinth.

Below
1   Timber support structure (89 x 38mm/3½ x 1½in).
2   18mm/¾in birch plywood painted matt on both sides.
3   18mm/¾in birch plywood laminated to 36mm/1½in (2 x 18mm/2 x ¾in).
4   Coloured laminate.
5   18mm/¾in birch plywood painted matt on both sides.
6   Timber support structure (89 x 38mm/3½ x 1½in).
7   Folded, powder-coated mild-steel light support.

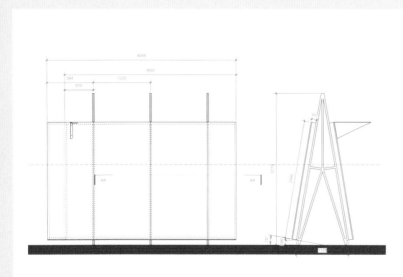

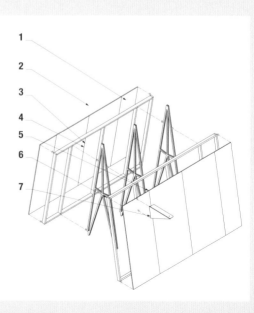

Above
Central frame junctions.

Above
A single-sided structure leans back on
the support structure for stability.

Below
1   Timber support structure (89 x 38mm/3½ x 1½in).
2   Timber stud structure (89 x 38mm/3½ x 1½in).
3   18mm/¾in Douglas Fir plywood, clear seal.
4   M16 nut, bolt and washer.

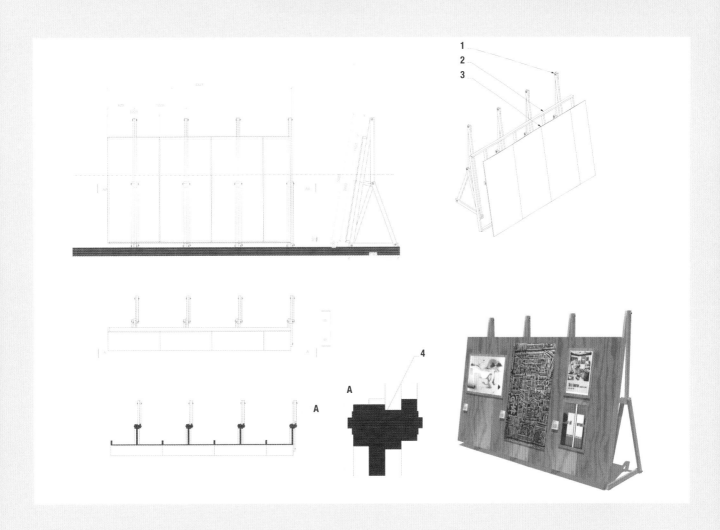

Left
The exhibition structure leans against the gallery wall and masks a ventilation grill and damaged floor tiles.

Below
1 Ventilation grill.
2 600 x 600mm/23½ x 23½in gallery floor tiles.
3 Supporting stud structure fixed to existing damaged floor tiles.
4 Gallery wall.
5 18mm/¾in birch plywood laminated to 36mm/1½in, matt varnish finish.
6 18mm/¾in MDF, matt varnish finish.
7 6mm/¼in clear acrylic.
8 Routed section for four maquettes, acrylic fronts flush with MDF.
9 6mm/¼in clear acrylic.
10 18mm/¾in MDF.
11 18mm/¾in MDF ZF back support.

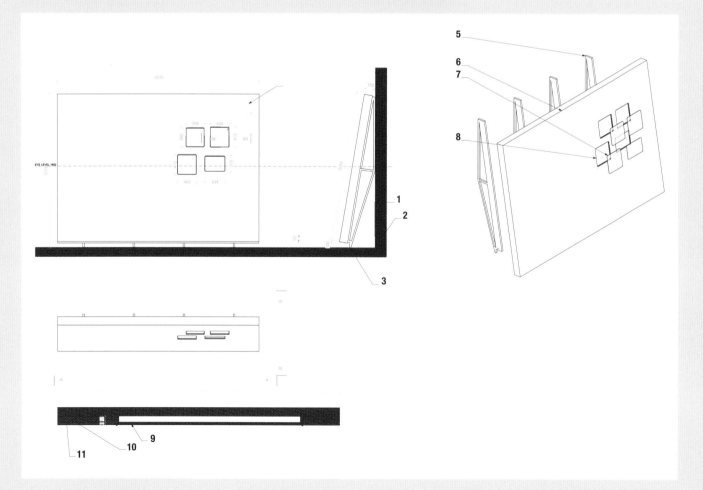

Left
The yellow triangular supports brace the shelf against the wall.

Below
Inclined wall shelf
1 6mm/¼in clear acrylic – mitred joints.
2 6mm/¼in birch plywood with sealed painted top surface.
3 Powder-coated folded mild steel.
4 Mild-steel graphics panel.
5 Powder-coated mild-steel support.
6 Powder-coated mild-steel support screwed to gallery wall.
7 Gallery wall.

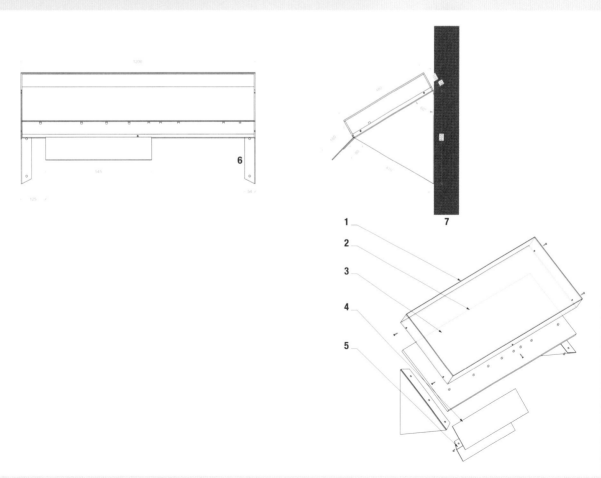

A Travelling Exhibition
Darwin Bicentennial – Arka Design

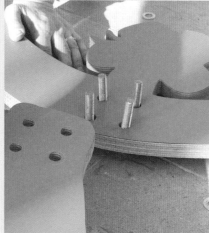

Above left to right
Parts for the 'tree' structure are unpacked…

…and bolted together…

CNC precision makes perfect housings
for other elements…

Right
…and slotted into position.

Travelling exhibitions present two challenges: they must look good and they should be easy to transport. Ideally they should also be adaptable to suit the variety of spaces – big, small and awkwardly shaped – into which they will be inserted. In this example, which was scheduled to travel the world, the base units provided stable groundings for the vertical panels and acted as containers for the smaller components during transportation between venues. CNC production gave great accuracy in the making of comparatively complex forms, like the 'trees', and great precision, and therefore rigidity, for the interlocking pieces. A wholly rigid connection is not possible since components must have enough leeway to slot together but uprights will gain stability if, as shown in the image opposite below they are slotted into both the top and bottom planes of the base structure.

Right
Intricate, mechanical interactive pieces.

Below
The travelling exhibition *in situ*.

Residential

Furniture for residential interiors must cater for a wide range of activity, from the social interaction of exuberant guests to the inertia of a single sleeper, and for the spectrum of clients' personal taste.

Designers will not be dealing with the rational expression of product values or the broad consensus of user expectation but directly with the individuals who will inhabit the interior, not for a brief visit but as the locus of their lives, who will expect a reflection of their aesthetic values, no matter how much at odds those might be with their designer's predilections. Designers may reasonably hope to be chosen because a client feels affinity for their work but, even where this is so, to create something in which the client is investing hope and expectation is difficult and sometimes inhibiting. The relationship between client and designer tends to become more personal than is normal in other projects. A consolation may sometimes be that the need to reconcile the very particular expectations of clients with the diversity of domestic functions will provoke designers to investigate unfamiliar options and add to their repertoire.

Domestic spaces are likely to be comparatively small and layouts of furniture within them may be prescribed by existing elements, windows, doors, heat sources. Often an intelligent arrangement of furniture can make sense of an awkward space defining how plans may be used. A substantial piece of furniture can define or subdivide an awkward area.

Residential clients who choose to have all their furniture designed and made are rare. If they do it is likely that they will want something that only a craftsman or craftswoman can supply and a designer must provide a context for that object. Reluctance in commissioning new pieces is likely to be financially motivated but equally likely to be the result of a wish to retain loved objects or to acquire aspirational manufactured pieces. In the last few decades as shops selling design-led furniture have proliferated clients have acquired a much greater awareness of what is available and firmer opinions about what they want. IKEA offers everyone an eclectic entry level experience of styles and standards, an introduction that may lead to more rarefied and expensive shops and showrooms Personal taste evolves further in public interiors, in cafés, bars, restaurants, hotels and shops that have been early adopters of contemporary design. A designer's role may be to orchestrate a client's selection or it may be to gauge underlying taste and to suggest, for consideration, other pieces that share the aesthetic. While a designer may be dogmatic about furniture for commercial interiors for which the client expects objective advice, residential clients themselves are likely to be intensely subjective and, if they are not, should be encouraged to become more personally involved in an environment that will be exclusively theirs. The designers' role may involve a significant element of counselling and, if there are pieces in the finished project that do not quite correspond to their taste, perhaps they should consider their job well done.

A client will not necessarily want new furniture but be willing to accept that existing pieces need to be upgraded to fit comfortably in a new context. This is particularly easy to achieve with upholstered pieces and particularly necessary because fabrics wear and fade.

Clients will often prize autobiographical possessions that hold more significance than the furniture on which they are displayed. While such predetermined selections may be difficult to integrate they also offer useful suggestions for design directions and, just as the quirks of an existing building can prompt invention, so furniture pieces by other imaginations can be inspirational.

Clients will often have esoteric possessions that have to be assimilated.

Furniture Defines Space

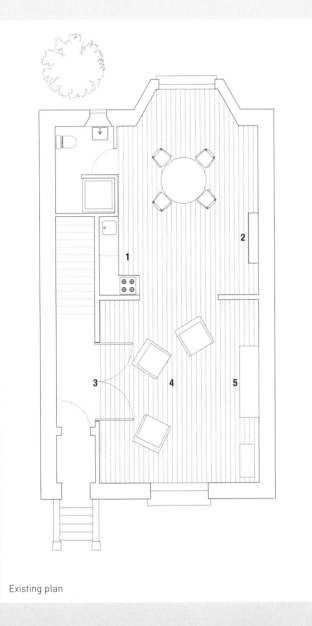

Existing plan

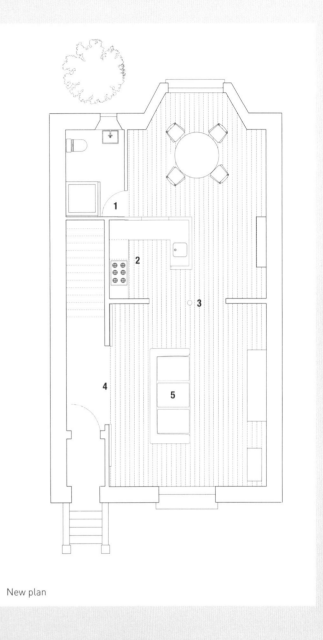

New plan

This project illustrates the value of creating a well-defined area for existing pieces of furniture (the table) and using a substantial new piece (the sofa) to define the circulation zone, from the entrance to the kitchen and dining areas, and to consolidate the sitting area. The realigned kitchen makes a circulation 'waist' that consolidates the parameters of the areas with direct access to views. The low wall that encloses it does not interfere with the sense of a single large space but is high enough to mask an untidy worktop.

Existing plan

1 Kitchen creates ill-defined central area.
2 Fireplace.
3 Double doors.
4 Armchairs 'float' in ill-defined area.
5 Fireplace.

New plan

1 Door moved to consolidate table position at window.
2 Kitchen increased in size and enclosed by 1200mm-/47¼in-high wall to 'inhabit' the amorphous central space. The windows are visible from the working area.
3 New round column to define kitchen area.
4 Sliding doors ease circulation.
5 Large sofa (2400 x 1000mm/94½ x 39¼in) consolidates the space in front of the fireplace.

Screens and dividers

Interior design frequently involves the subdivision of existing spaces. The construction techniques for solid, floor-to-ceiling, wall-to-wall lightweight partitions have been refined to provide the quickest and most efficient method of making a cellular interior, but not all projects require such definitive subdivision. Less comprehensive separation is often called for, to define discrete areas while maintaining awareness of the whole.

Pieces of furniture may be designed exclusively to divide and define but frequently they have a secondary function, most often for storage, since shelving, cupboards and cabinets are easily configured to suit particular locations. They also offer the opportunity to introduce a more diverse palette of materials and detailing techniques than those employed in the making of standard partitions.

Openings, glazed or unglazed, may be inserted into solid walls to introduce a sense of separation

Below
A proprietary suspended, perforated screen of green plastic components acts as demarcation between two office areas. High-backed seating separates workspace from corridor.

rather than isolation. This may be easily accomplished with adjustments to the framing pattern of a stud partition. Solid partitions may stop short of floor or ceiling but construction becomes more complicated. All variations on standard stud partitions retain a sense of solidity, which will be desirable for particular solutions. But where something less substantial is required the techniques of furniture making are more effective. It is appropriate to classify as furniture a partition that is constructed using the machinery and materials, timber and timber derivatives, metals, glass and plastics more normally used in furniture making.

Furniture pieces may be built into solid walls. While they normally take on a storage role as cupboards or shelves, they can also fulfil any of the conventional functions of furniture, as chairs, tables or beds. The insertion of cupboards or shelving, accessible from both sides but with opaque back panels, will relieve a flat wall plane. Shelves open to both sides will provide a visual link. These may require vertical subdivision to reduce their span or for aesthetic pattern-making. Since they are unlikely to have been conceived for practical reasons, this will be the primary consideration.

Above
Booths separate areas
within a staff restaurant.

Below
1 A thin wall without top support will fall over.
2 Walls with wider bases will be more stable the greater X is in relation to Y.
3 The wall will be vulnerable because it is asymmetrical – the foot portion could be fixed to the floor, but this will put stress on the junction of vertical and horizontal. If the vertical is connected with the centre of the horizontal, the weight distribution would improve but the strength of the junction would remain critical.
4 The wall is strong because the width reduces with height and the centre of gravity is low, with weight concentrated at the base.

In **5**, X (the width of the base) is defined by the extremities of the curves. An angled plan would satisfy the same principle.
In **6**, X is again defined by the extremities of the curve and the broader sweep better distributes the load.

Such furniture pieces will normally be prefabricated off site and inserted into apertures left in the new partitions. It is risky to construct even a lightweight stud partition around a furniture element since damage to delicate arrises is likely. The opening in the wall must be built accurately but with a tolerance of 5mm to allow the piece to be put in position. The junction between furniture and wall can be covered with a thin length of timber that covers the joint, or emphasized by a 'shadow gap', a narrow recess, typically 10mm wide, between the edge of the wall opening and the furniture piece. A storage or display element inserted into a wall is likely to be deeper than the 100–125mm of the standard stud partition. The furniture piece may project beyond the wall plane or the wall may be built with two parallel stud frames to match or exceed its depth.

There is no reason why a furniture piece that extends from floor to ceiling and between walls should not incorporate a door opening. Dividers, however, are likely to stop short of ceiling level and may not touch any walls. Such freestanding pieces are potentially unstable, particularly when their height is significantly greater than their depth. Fixing to the floor will add some stability, but the taller the piece, the greater the rotational stress on connections. There are a number of ways to achieve stability. Connections may be made to a secure fixing at

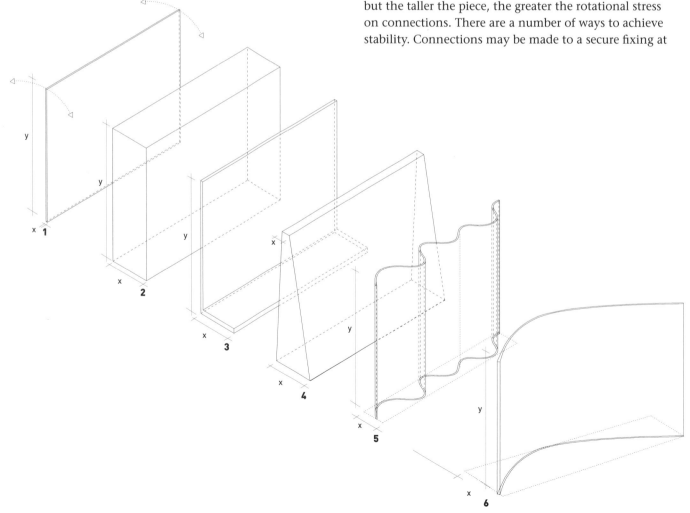

y

y

x **1**

x **2**

x **3**

y

x **4**

y

x **5**

y

x **6**

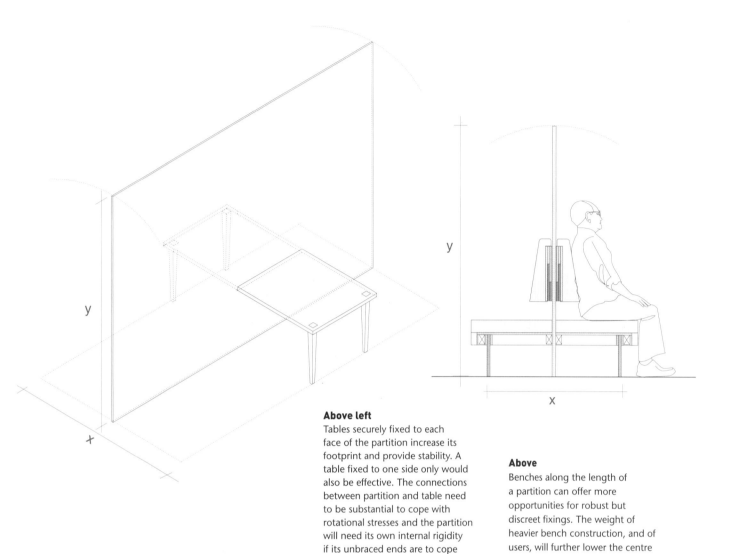

Above left
Tables securely fixed to each
face of the partition increase its
footprint and provide stability. A
table fixed to one side only would
also be effective. The connections
between partition and table need
to be substantial to cope with
rotational stresses and the partition
will need its own internal rigidity
if its unbraced ends are to cope
with applied loading and impact.

Above
Benches along the length of
a partition can offer more
opportunities for robust but
discreet fixings. The weight of
heavier bench construction, and of
users, will further lower the centre
of gravity.

ceiling level. With a suspended ceiling, particularly one of lightweight acoustic panels set on a grid frame hung on wires, top or 'head' fixings must be made to the structural floor slab above ceiling level. If the vertical connecting members are comparatively slim, metal rather than timber, and visibly different from the finished surface of the divider itself, then their presence will be insignificant.

If the width of the divider is increased and its weight is concentrated at the base, then its centre of gravity will be lowered and its resistance to overturning increased. The nominal width of a thin divider will be increased if its plan incorporates angles or curves. Set out carelessly, these may consume an unacceptably large area of the floor, but with intelligent planning they can be organized to define usable spaces on either side of the divider or to incorporate other furniture elements. Seats, tables or low-level cupboards attached to a divider can act as stabilizing outriggers.

Screens and divisions can incorporate power and lighting effectively if consideration is given to the circulation of wiring and the incorporation of fittings

from the earliest design stages. A piece that is a grid of thin components will pose problems but it is possible to integrate exposed wiring or the conduit in which it runs convincingly into the overall composition. If it cannot be wholly concealed then it is better to treat it frankly, choose a visually acceptable cable and incorporate as a component in the composition.

The precision of detailing necessary to produce a successful dividing element will normally mean that it will be most successfully prefabricated in a specialist workshop and it is important to ensure that what is likely to be an awkwardly shaped and heavy object can be manoeuvred through access routes to the interior during delivery to site. It may be necessary to consider how the complete piece can be dismantled or divided into manageable sections for delivery to site. The most satisfactory solution is to devise joints that are hidden from view after installation or identical to other elements, performing other roles, that are visible in the assembled piece.

Temporary Screen / Temporary Store
Archivo de Creadores de Madrid – El Ultimo Grito

Interior planning is fundamentally about assigning activities to spaces but the configuration of the dividing element defines the nature of the boundary between one area and another. Solid partitions are clear statements of territory but the relative permeability of a screen is inviting.

A composite of several furniture pieces defines a consultation space within a temporary exhibition. Its structure incorporates shelving and a table to provide stabilizing weight and lateral stiffening.

Below
The solid image-wall floats on a red-painted tubular metal base. Wheels confirm its transitory nature.

Above

The panels that make up the partition are joined and stiffened by a timber frame, which in turn is supported and stiffened by the tubular metal frame that also supports the shelves, which contribute counterbalancing weight. The attached table provides additional stability.

Left

The wooden frame of the table and screening box contribute significant weight to counterbalance the wall. The expedient construction of the lighting support is in sympathy with the elegant rationality of the whole.

Permanent Barrier / Permanent Desk
University Library – Nomad

This bench, which acts as a low but wholly effective division between the library area proper and social/.group learning spaces, is designed to gather together all the self-service equipment in the library: search terminals, self-issue machines, printers and copiers. The complexity of the collected equipment, and the provision of integrated seating for those waiting, generates a number of different units that share a modular structure and materials palette.

Above
The 'utility bench' marks the boundary between social/group learning and more conventional library accommodation beyond.

Below left
Copying
1 Photocopier.
2 25mm-/1in-deep foam on 10mm/½in plywood, upholstered in Bute tweed fabric.
3 25mm-/1in-deep foam on 10mm/½in plywood, upholstered in Bute tweed fabric.
4 15mm-/½in-deep x 50mm-/2in-high shadow gap faced with 'Polyrey' wood veneer laminate.
5 15mm-/½in-deep x 50mm-/2in-high shadow gap faced with 'Polyrey' wood veneer.

Below middle
Self-issue
1 'Opac' search.
2 Stainless-steel cable grommet with rubber gasket.
3 10mm/½in plywood carcass clad with 12mm/½in plywood faced with Formica laminate. Hardwood edges to be sprayed to match.
4 10mm/½in plywood cupboard doors faced with Formica laminate.
5 Routed finger pull on top edge of cupboard doors. Cupboard lock in shadow gap.

Below right
Help station/printing
1 Printer.
2 Two-person help station.
3 10mm/½in plywood cupboard doors faced with Formica laminate.
4 'Polyrey' wood laminate shadow gap with routed finger channel top and bottom to open doors. Cupboard lock in shadow gap.
5 Cable routes formed in carcass.
6 'Polyrey' wood veneer.

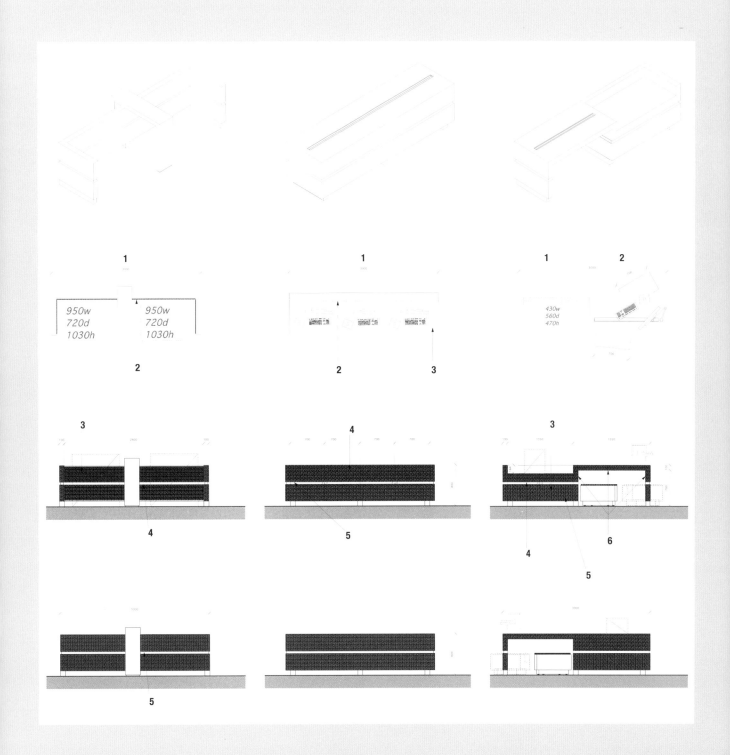

950w
720d
1030h

950w
720d
1030h

430w
560d
470h

Below
Bright, spray-painted MDF shelves
and drawers are integrated
into the black oriented strand
board (OSB) partitions.

Storage

Storage furniture may be broadly divided into that which is built into the fabric of the interior and that which is freestanding. Some of the latter may be, or should be, mobile in response to the changes digital technology has brought to office life, where workers are no longer confined to a designated desk space. Digital technology has made information-retrieval faster and simpler, but it has not eliminated the need for paper copies of crucial correspondence and hard copies of transactions and agreements.

Cupboards or cabinets with shelves and drawers are readily available, mass-produced in a diversity of materials and configurations, so there is seldom a justification for producing one-off pieces. However, there are particular contexts and activities that warrant project-specific solutions when standard pieces may not align aesthetically. In others, the nature and condition of the items to be stored may require particular provision. When a high level of environmental control is necessary, it is prudent to specify specialist storage units and, where the intent is storage rather than display, appearance will not be a primary consideration.

In most interiors, most long-term storage can be accommodated in the small and often oddly shaped rooms that remain when the principal rooms have been created. If accessible, well-lit and damp-free, the latter will satisfy the requirements of most small and medium-sized organizations. Where possible, storage-room dimensions should be multiples of those of standard equipment to ensure the most effective use of space. If a length of wall is an aggregate of the width of a standard filing cabinet, which is itself determined by standard paper sizes, corners to attract rubbish will be eliminated. If the space between the edge of an architrave and the nearest corner is enough to accommodate the depth of a filing cabinet, the opening door will not eliminate cabinet positions. If the planning process is to respond precisely to specified pieces, it is important to check that details of the equipment and details of construction are compatible. Ideally storage furniture should have a plinth recessed on its rear face so that a skirting does not prevent its sitting tight against the wall. The dimensions of a plinth recess should be checked against both the projection and height of the skirting. There are seldom recesses on the side of a standard plinth, so the crucial dimension to ensure a fit on plan is that between skirtings rather than walls. It is, however, acceptable to remove skirtings behind and to the side of storage units to achieve a tight fit since the storage equipment will then perform the role of the skirting, protecting the base of walls from impact damage. Corners of rooms are seldom precisely right-angled, and even if the pieces will fit snugly along the back wall an acute angle can eliminate one cabinet. It is therefore advisable to check angles and to allow a tolerance gap of at least 10mm/½in between skirtings.

When frequently used, storage furniture must be sited close to those who need it rather than in a separate enclosed area; it then becomes a visually significant component in the interior and specification of the right model becomes a crucial design decision. There are two broad categories of choice: metal shells, available in a limited range of bland colours; and wooden shells, which are finished in a range of bland mid-brown veneers. Manufacturers aim to maximize their market and work on the presumption that a self-effacing product will work for most buyers who are interested in economical and proven solutions. Clients have largely come to accept as inevitable the visual intrusion of storage pieces and it takes very minor deviations from mundane and familiar options to provoke a positive response. For the interior designer dissatisfied with the standard products, there are two options: to customize them or to integrate them.

Customizing involves the repainting of metal shells and the replacement of wooden veneers. Both necessarily involve substantial extra costs as a high standard of specialist work is required to match the finish of factory-made products. The more familiar and perhaps the more mundane the object, the more compelling its transformation will be. It may be possible to find second-hand examples for refurbishment but it may also be difficult to find sufficient numbers of identical models. Sometimes it may be possible to make a virtue of second-hand pieces in their own right. Recycling distressed secondhand equipment is always a solution to limited budgets and deemed virtuous.

Integration involves choosing a piece or range of furniture and using it as the starting point for subsequent decisions about finishes for the interior in which it stands. It is much easier to select a paint colour that will complement a proprietary piece than to find one that will work effectively with a preselected decorative scheme. Strictly complementary finishes need only be used for the immediate context of a piece and the other areas can evolve from those.

Integration may be taken a step further if new pieces are housed in purpose-built recesses, which may be existing idiosyncrasies of the plan fine-tuned to suit the dimensions of the new piece or pockets built into new partition walls.

Storage in retail is more ambiguous than in offices. While there are back-of-house storage areas, there is also a significant capacity, particularly in self-service shops, for storage on the sales floor, which, as it is depleted by customers, is replenished by staff. The more efficiently this is carried out, the greater the turnover of goods as popular items are constantly made available.

Replacement goods are held in storage areas that are accessed only by staff. Such areas need be no more than practical. Dimensions should be appropriate to the goods on sale and organization should make the act of locating individual items easy. Assistants searching for products in response to a customer request need to know where to go and, if an item can't be found, need to be confident that they have checked the only area in which it might be stored. If they spend too long in the storeroom, the sales floor will be short-staffed, customers will grow frustrated and security will be reduced. Digital stock control, which keeps constantly updated records of stock, increasingly renders abortive trips to storage areas unnecessary.

Display furniture on sales floors can incorporate storage, both of a secure nature or of a kind that can be freely accessed by customers. Some products, like food in a supermarket or clothes in a high-street chain, should be available for spontaneous scrutiny by customers, regardless of the destruction visited on well-presented displays. Open shelves, plinths and rails will most effectively meet functional requirements and the simpler their form, the more effectively they will present products and the more crucial will be their detailing. Proportions and detailing will contribute to customers' perception of the product but this is not an argument for elitist design solutions. The best retail designers work to communicate with and persuade shoppers rather than to win the approval of their peers.

Below
Standard sizes for lockers in the staffroom and filing cabinets in the office determine the locations of new partitions.

1 Kitchen.
2 Wash-up space.
3 Staff changing.
4 Office.
5 Plant room.
6 Storage space.

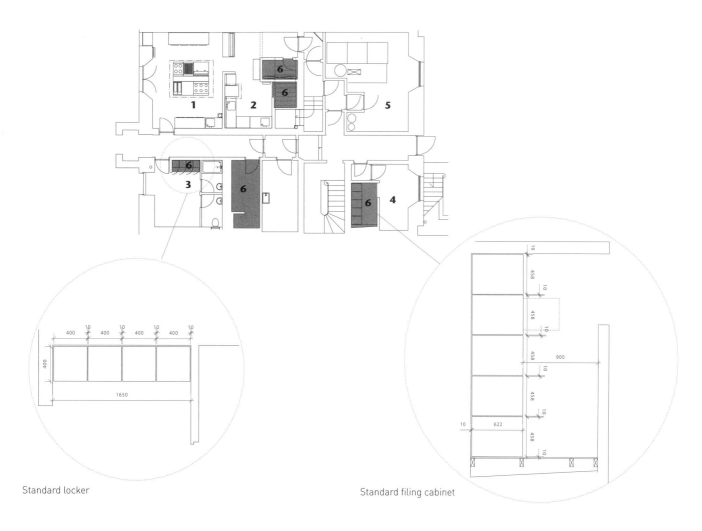

Standard locker

Standard filing cabinet

Making good

Projections and indentations on an existing wall may be eliminated completely by a length of stud-framed wall but practical good sense can often recognize opportunities for built-in storage or seating within the voids created between the new unbroken length of wall and the irregularities of the old. Often no more is required than a range of doors to close off shelves and drawers set within the three sides of a recess or the seat and back of a built-in bench to occupy its width. However, existing corners are seldom right angles or the depth of a recess

constant, so detailed measurement on site is essential and expedient alteration on site often necessary.

There are often hidden voids in any interior that may be exploited for storage. The most common are the hollow cores of stud partition walls. Although offering depths of only 75mm/3in or 100mm/4in, they can be useful for storing the small objects that get lost at the back of conventional cupboards. The vertical studs at 400mm/16¾in or 600mm/23½in centres can determine door locations.

Right
Eliminating an uneven existing wall and inserting storage or display units.

A Existing plan:
Wall A has a number of irregular projections and an angled section.

B New plan:
A new stud partition makes a single wall plane.

C Existing elevation:
Showing projections, pipe and electrical control box and surface-mounted conduit.

D The wall may be left as a single plane and painted. It can conceal new electrical cabling and plumbing pipes.

E Prefabricated plywood or MDF niches and boxes can be inserted into the new wall plane to occupy the voids between it and the original. The vertical row of square boxes can only have the depth of the stud framing, which separates the new wall face from the existing.

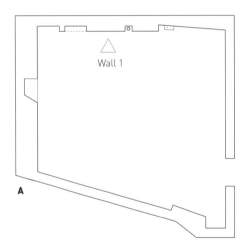

A

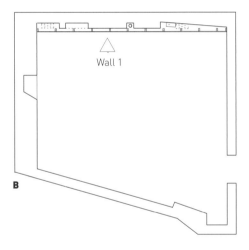

B

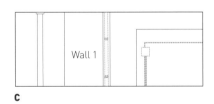

C

D

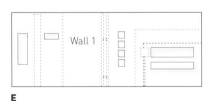

E

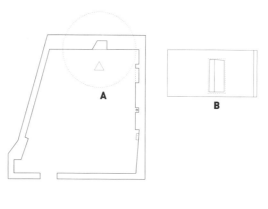

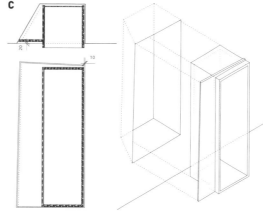

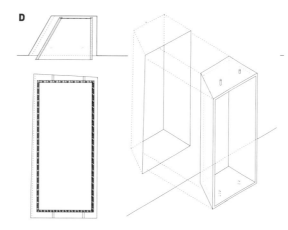

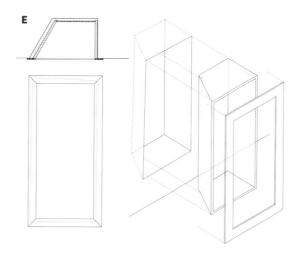

Above

The void can also be exploited for display. In this example open-ended 300 x 300 x 125mm/11¾ x 11¾ x 5in MDF boxes are inserted into the core of a plasterboard partition with 88mm stud framework. The box sits tight against the back face of the plasterboard on the other side of the partition, which becomes the back face of the niche.

Left

Inserting a cupboard into an irregular recess.

A Existing plan showing recess B.

B Elevation with recess B.

C Option 1:
The cupboard carcass is set in the recess and a plywood or MDF collar, scribed to fit the non-rectangular opening, is inserted to close off gaps. The collar may be fixed flush with the face of the wall or, more efficiently, set back behind the face. Minor gaps to the existing wall can be filled.

D Option 2:
The cupboard carcass may be made to match the angles of the recess on the plan. The edges and top will not necessarily be exactly vertical and horizontal, and tolerance gaps should be allowed all around. The carcass can sit behind, flush with or in front of the wall. The gaps can be sealed as in option 1. If left open, the gap at floor level should be enough to allow cleaning.

E Option 3:
As option 2, but the front of the carcass is set level with the face of the wall and architrave strips cover gaps. Minor gaps between architraves and an uneven wall can be filled.

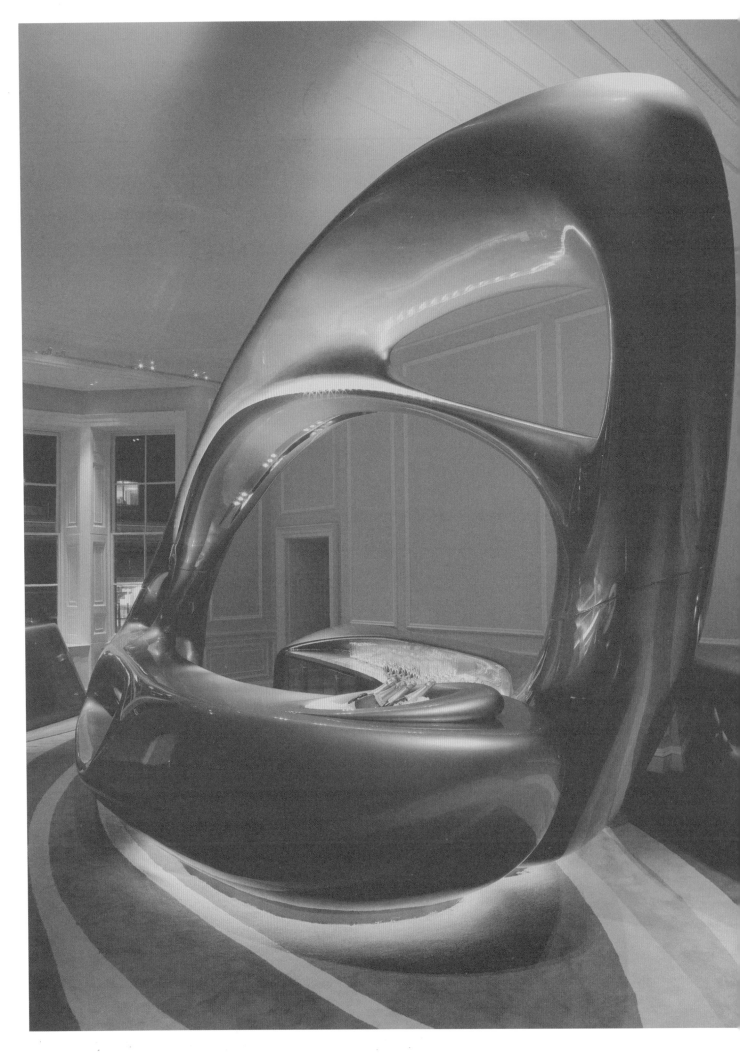

PART 2 TYPES OF FURNITURE

Off the shelf

Certain generic pieces of furniture are of such fundamental importance to the conduct of our daily lives that they are mass-produced. Their basic configurations, on which we sit and sleep, work and eat, are defined by the rules of anthropometrics and ergonomics, and manufacturers, competing for their share of what has become a global market, offer a plethora of stylistic embellishments of

practical armatures. To the new pieces brought to market every year, whether with a fanfare at international furniture exhibitions or introduced more discreetly into the ranges on offer in retail chains, must be added the popular products of previous years whose profitability ensures their continuous production.

This page
Modern 'classics', such as the Eames' white fibreglass 'La Chaise' (top) and white leather lounge chair and ottoman, may be given a supportive context by complementary contemporary pieces.

Left
Plywood and chrome elegance
from 1952 – the designer's café
chair of choice.

Artist: Jacobsen, Arne (1902-1971)
Title: Chair Serie 7, 3107, 1952
Location: Museum of Modern Art (MoMA)
City: New York
Country: USA
Period/Style: Not available
Genre: Design
Note: Chrome-plated steel tubing and
molded plywood with black lacquer. Each:
30 1/4 x 18 x 20' (76.8 x 45.7 x 50.8 cm).
Gift of Mr. Jacques and Mrs. Anna B. Dutka.
Acc.n.: 24.1997.1-2
Credits:Digital image, The Museum of
Modern Art, New York/Scala, Florence

It is unlikely that a designer creating an interior need look beyond manufacturers' catalogues for tables and chairs. In public interiors particularly – workplaces, bars and restaurants – the regulations governing dimensions, configurations, standards of construction and fire resistance are best dealt with by specialist designers and manufacturers. Mass-producers can more easily absorb the costs of the prototype testing that is necessary to make a successful marriage of aesthetic intentions and practical obligations. On another practical level, it is also unlikely that the costs of developing a successful version of an object as familiar but as complex as a chair can be absorbed within the design fee for a single interior. And it is probably true to say that pieces by specialist furniture designers are more comfortable, albeit sometimes at the expense of aesthetic purity, than those by architects and designers that are designated 'iconic' and are rushed to production, while their creator's name has commercial currency. Gerrit Rietveld's 'Red Blue' chair of *c.* 1923 is a notorious example of concept triumphing over function. Few who own one sit on it, other than to demonstrate that it is possible – if painful – to do so. It is kept as evidence of insider taste, or as the equivalent of a pet.

Rather than setting out to create new pieces, it is more usual, and usually more efficient, for designers to build their awareness of what is available in the wholesale and retail markets. Just as they tend to evolve a personal aesthetic language that is the foundation of all their work, so they tend to adopt a few pieces that complement their other signature gestures. While this may project something of the glamour of a personal 'vision', it is not necessarily to be applauded, either in the design of the whole or the selection of the parts, since it can result in

the imposition of familiar solutions on unfamiliar contexts that deserve their own consideration. There are certain pieces, Arne Jacobsen's 'Series 7' chair, for example, that are universally approved by the design community; to choose them is to declare allegiance to the pack. The more interesting designers are more likely to avoid such elegant clichés.

To avoid predictable solutions, designers have to make themselves aware of new pieces as they appear, and this, in turn, may prompt fresh thinking about the other elements in their work. The process of adding to an established furniture repertoire, which once relied on the time-consuming compilation and continuous updating of a physical archive of brochures that were quick to collect dust, is another beneficiary of digital technology. An online search, as wide or as focused by materials, context, price, manufacturer or specialist designer as necessary, presents the range of global options for consideration. This generosity, and accessibility, of choice has inevitably broadened palettes and encouraged eclecticism. The instinct that prompted designers to impose a singular vision defined by a few prescribed pieces has softened, and larger spaces are increasingly furnished with a spectrum of diverse but compatible pieces that add up to a more interesting and occasionally provocative whole.

Choice will frequently be determined by price and, as with every other purchase, it is generally true that the greater the amount of money spent, the more elegant the object bought and the better the quality of materials and production. There are expensive exceptions to this general rule, objects that are unlikely to be included in any designer's canon of acceptability but which, if they survive in the marketplace, may be assumed to have

Top
Disparate pieces, broadly domestic in character, all on the borderline of acceptable taste but all with cultural resonance, sit among utilitarian columns and glazed partitions under a moulded metal-tiled ceiling.

Above
A rich collection of pieces define areas within a hotel atrium.

a legitimacy and a cultural resonance that warrants 'ironic' selection. The most expensive pieces are usually those designated 'classics' of modern design. They are principally objects, usually chairs, that are spin-offs from the domestic interiors created by the revered early exponents of Modernism, the stainless-steel frames and leather upholstery of Le Corbusier with Charlotte Perriand, of Mies van der Rohe with Lilly Reich, the bentwood pieces of Hans Wegner and Alvar Aalto, the plastic, metal and plywood composites of Charles and Ray Eames. Most continue to be bought for domestic interiors but some, like Mies's 'Barcelona' chair and Charles and Ray Eames's office chairs, have become familiar within hotel lobbies and offices as signifiers of corporate taste and status. 'Classics' have a cachet that may speak to other designers rather more than it does to clients and those who use their buildings. It has, however, been argued that the eternal visual qualities of a successful Modernist classic enable it to sit comfortably within a traditional interior and evidence would suggest that time reconciles lay users to objects that were once iconoclastic.

All 'classics' (which also include pieces by, among others, Charles Rennie Mackintosh, Frank Lloyd Wright, Eileen Gray and Arne Jacobsen) when manufactured under licence to the specifications of the original, with some minor adjustments made in deference to modern machine production and legislation, have a certified pedigree and carry a premium price. Wholly convincing facsimiles – often described, to circumvent the letter if not the spirit of copyright law, as 'inspired by' the original – are available at a fraction of the price of 'genuine' reproductions. Their specification is likely to be prompted by a client's reluctance to spend excessively and a designer's willingness to disregard licensing agreements. Given the egalitarian principles declared by Modernist pioneers, they might perhaps be gratified that their work is now widely accessible. The morality of reproducing work still under copyright is more questionable since the creator is likely to be alive and in some degree dependent on royalty payments. First editions, battered as they may be, are collectors' items and priced accordingly, far in excess of even the most legitimate later productions. Once acquired, they are more likely to be treated as exhibits, deserving curatorial care, rather than as functioning objects.

More modest pieces creatively chosen to complement their context can have as much impact as the most expensive pieces and are perhaps, lacking status of their own, more likely to make a self-effacing contribution to a coherent whole.

Right
The Eameses' 'Soft Pad Chaise' of 1946 by Charles and Ray Eames. Given its form and material palette, it is inevitably reminiscent of the 1928 chaise longue by Le Corbusier and his female collaborator, Charlotte Perriand.

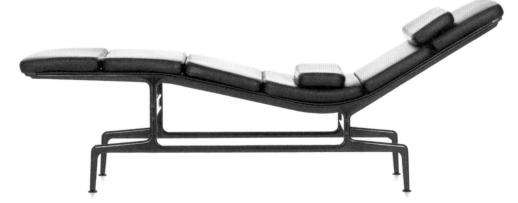

Far left
Ludwig Mies van der Rohe and Lilly Reich's chair was designed for the German Pavilion at the 1929 International Exposition in Barcelona. It is worth noting that Lilly Reich is now credited as the major influence behind Mies's furniture designs, which points to the importance of the contribution made by specialists.

Left
The colours and pattern of this woven bamboo chair sit comfortably with existing floor tiles.

Reuse and recycling

Existing pieces may be retained to sit unobtrusively within interior shells in which little other intervention has been made or to perform as counterpoints within radical conversions. Modestly worn upholstery fabrics can add patina. Excessively worn fabrics that need to be replaced with new ones offer the opportunity to combine pristine contemporary textiles with imperfect exposed frames and traditional well-stuffed forms. Those who know about such things will be interested in, if not necessarily approving of, the mixing of periods and styles. Those who do not are likely to enjoy the diversity.

When a decision has been made to use recycled pieces, luck and intelligent selection in junk and antique shops, specialist reclamation yards, flea markets and real and virtual auction rooms offer designers unanticipated components with which to orchestrate their solutions. No find will match expectations exactly but an unexpected piece can stimulate the imagination. While

Left
Comparatively recent objects can be as extraordinary as period pieces.

Below
A good junk shop poses multiple questions of choice. Collections are as easily discovered as single pieces.

Far left
Draping existing pieces is the simplest way to upgrade. This example is particularly good because the fabric is generous enough to make relaxed folds and loose knots, which are embellished by the exposing of existing embroidery. The grey-blue cloth that shows beneath the white connects with painted floor and cushion and confirms that this is not a dust sheet but a permanent solution.

Left
Paint applied with spontaneity and minimal deliberation will best cope with reclaimed pieces in poor condition. A broken and mottled finish will camouflage damaged surfaces. A smooth, carefully applied finish will draw attention to detail.

Left
The colour matching of upholstery fabric and wall paint (the yellow and blue cushions relate to paint colours on the opposite wall) make this refurbished sofa the crucial element in the room. It is always wise to choose the fabric first since it is easier to match paint colours than to have fabric custom dyed. Digital printing of cloth and wallpaper opens up interesting possibilities for matching patterns.

it is comparatively simple to find a single or a modest matching collection of second-hand pieces for a small-scale project, it is unlikely that enough identical pieces will be found to furnish cafés, offices or other multi-occupancy spaces. In such circumstances the solution and the challenge is to assemble disparate examples, singly or in batches, to exploit varying aesthetic and cultural resonances to offer different but comprehensible readings. Usually. the greater the diversity, the easier it is to achieve coherence – which can be characterized by the very lack of consistency. Diverse styles can be unified if all pieces are painted in the same or tonally compatible colours. Loose cushions that share a fabric will bring coherence to a disparate collection of chairs.

Left
In the Jellyfish Theatre, in south London, benches are made from mundane materials with expedient techniques. That the chair seat and back are fixed to the bench base confirms that the intention is frivolous. The remnants of boards and veneers fixed casually to the wall conform to the aesthetic.

Below
Clothing familiar objects transforms them and unifies the room.

Right
Conventional objects can be transformed by draperies and loose covers, which may be useful in restaurants, where spilt food can decommission upholstered chairs.

A first instinct may be to look for the grander second-hand pieces, but these are predictable and probably expensive to buy, adapt or repair. In a restricted space they are likely to appropriate a disproportionate amount of space. More utilitarian pieces can have as much impact because they confound expectations, but whatever the status of recycled and redeployed pieces, they are obliged to function as efficiently as those that are new and purpose-made. Incongruity may excuse a degree of functional compromise but that must be minimized. There are optimum dimensions and an acceptable degree of comfort for every piece which are determined by its function. Quirky chairs in a workplace, which vary even slightly from the optimum dimensions, or which have awkwardly placed arms and do not swivel, will undermine efficiency and may cause injuries. A sofa may be popular with café customers but it will hold comparatively few of them in relation to the floor space it occupies. Equally, it may be awkwardly low for those who are eating but comfortable enough to make them reluctant to leave to make space for newcomers who are ready to spend. Hard chairs and unsteady tables may be appropriately picturesque but are likely to discourage customers from making a return visit.

An advantage of the down-at-heel piece is that refurbishment need not necessarily be carried out with finesse. A battered frame will accept an upholstery fabric that is stapled rather than stitched in position, and replacing a broken leg with one that is a different material and style is perfectly acceptable, as is the well-tried expedient of painting one or all of the legs of tables and chairs in different colours, just to make it clear that the original piece is not to be taken too seriously. A perfectly applied single paint colour across a collection of non-matching pieces will create a monotone celebration of form. A roughly daubed finish will disguise blemishes and suggest that imperfections are to be enjoyed.

If intact pieces can be visually deconstructed or reconstructed by painting, it is also possible to create new objects by assembling all or some parts of found pieces, to make a functioning three-dimensional collage. Again, the result will depend on available originals and the designer's ability to see and realize possibilities. Refined transitions between pieces are unlikely to be possible, more expedient conjunctions will be in the spirit of the whole. Standard dimensions for generic pieces offer a degree of crude compatibility. The mundane nature of original pieces will make their composite conclusion the more extraordinary.

Left
The timber textures and simple four-square form of the purpose-built wooden base supports the smooth, curved plastic of the pivoting seat shell appropriated from an Eames dining chair.

Below
In shops salvaged and recycled objects can provide counterpoints that enhance the products on display.

Above
Found objects can be 'tuned' to deal with new functions. The ball on the end of the roughly finished hanging rail, which is screwed to the timber of a salvaged pulley, prevents hangers from sliding off.

Right
Parquet flooring, salvaged from the original floor, faces the bar and banquette seating of this upgraded café. Foam cushions are covered in salvaged fabrics.

Right

The emphatic grain of the timber veneer and the angles of the table and window piers are echoed in the suspended ceiling pieces.

Far right

The profligate use of the red stools, the only coloured objects in this all-white space, defines the room. The length of the white-stained timber table, emphasized by the central joint in its top, contributes to the particularity of the space.

Right

Robustly solid pieces sit well in the glazed hotel reception area, once an outdoor space. The high percentage of 'modern classics' by Le Corbusier and Mies van der Rohe imply status.

Time and Place
Oilily – Uxus Design

While such improvisations using recycled material may be most appropriate to domestic interiors or bars and hotels, they can be deployed anywhere under the right circumstances. A children's clothes shop obviously offers a context for whimsical adaptation.

A knowledge of – or a willingness to search for – current mass-produced components, such as ironmongery, shelving systems and lighting fixtures, will provide compatible parts that will enhance and unify ad hoc compositions.

Right
A stack of miscellaneous chairs, linked for stability and painted to lighten the dark brown wood, becomes a display unit.

Below
A wardrobe is converted into a changing room. Some elements, like the red step, are inserted to accommodate the drawers, while others, like the entrance cut through the existing door leaf, remain stubbornly aloof.

Bespoke

While any piece of furniture in any interior may be designed specifically for its context, there are pieces, particular to each generic category of interior, that tend, almost always, to be designed as one-off, site-specific objects, because their role is to provide the interior with a distinctive identity. This may be achieved by producing a piece that draws on the language of the interior as a whole and which recedes modestly into the whole, or it may be a more flamboyant gesture that performs as a counterpoint to the comparatively more modest elements that enclose it. In the latter case, a designer may legitimately aspire to produce the extraordinary for its own sake. Different categories of interior require different degrees of gesture, dependent on their role. Modest interiors and activities deserve modest solutions: the effective solution does not depend on gratuitous extravagance but creative intelligence. Existing building shells, if they have any intrinsic qualities or any idiosyncrasies that merit retention, will have some influence on the furniture used in them, whether bespoke or off-the-shelf. The nature of the activity they accommodate will be equally influential: staid activities do not require flamboyance.

The particularities of building shells may preclude the use of the off-the-shelf solutions that are adequately equipped to meet prosaic practical needs efficiently and economically and something site specific will be required. While a good designer will always relish the opportunity to create something unique, extravagant gestures are likely to be inappropriate both conceptually and economically.

Whether a bespoke piece is extremely simple or extremely complex, its success will depend on the consistency of the thinking that conceives and shapes it and the quality of its making. Designers are likely to venture into new territories when pursuing the potential of a bespoke piece, considering the use of unfamiliar materials and unfamiliar making techniques. Seek specialist input from manufacturers and experienced makers as soon as such a possibility begins to emerge. Their knowledge will reduce research time and their scepticism will encourage pragmatism. Generally manufacturers are enthusiastic about opening up new ways of using their products; good makers will welcome new challenges.

The folded metal façade of this bar counter, which rises to ceiling level and runs the length of the restaurant behind, is the defining element of the interior. Its colours respond to the brick and stone of the original shell.

Left
Seating slides out on stout metal arms from below the thick, wooden block table, inspired by the chopping table in a traditional butcher's shop, that forms a spine running the length of this diner.

Above
Nominally a planter, this piece exploits the malleability, colours and patterns of solid core acrylic.

Right
This temporary bar in a trade show is constructed out of stretch fabric tensioned over wooden dowels that project from a timber substructure.

Counterpoint
Home House, private club – Zaha Hadid Architects

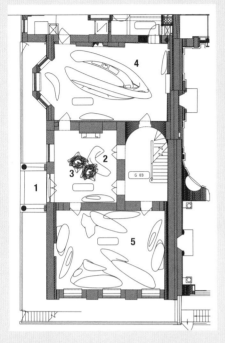

Above
1   Entrance.
2   Reception desk.
3   Chandelier over.
4   Bar.
5   Lounge.

Above right
The mass of the reception desk appears to sit lightly on the floor and its colour has perhaps some affinity with that of the existing walls. The desk anticipates the form of the bar beyond the open doorway.

Right
Practical equipment forms an armature for the counter.

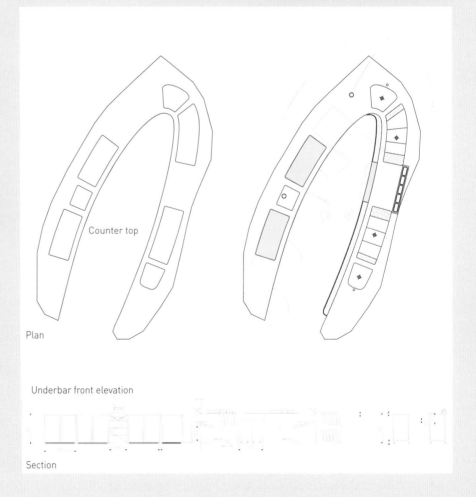

Counter top

Plan

Underbar front elevation

Section

Here a reception desk and a bar counter make no attempt to conform to the visual language of the restoration in the traditional rooms where they sit but their singular presences declare the building's change of use, from grand town house to private club.

With their bulbous forms, which curve back under them, they appear to sit lightly on the floor. The form begun in the reception desk evolves, becoming bigger and more complex for the bar counter beneath which an elliptical carpet acts as a further distancing device. The spotlights focused on the highly reflective surfaces of both compound their alien nature.

The plans of the bar counter show that the equipment, which is essential to the smooth operation of any bar, has been slotted into an unsympathetic carapace and the sequencing of its layout contributes to its efficient operation. As in any other island counter, even the more utilitarian equipment that is normally concealed behind the raised front of a more conventional single-aspect counter is all visible to some of the customers who line its perimeter, which makes refinement of detailing the more important. The more outrageous the proposal, the greater the detailing challenge. Any practical shortcomings will add credence to whatever attack potential critics may wish to make on aesthetic grounds.

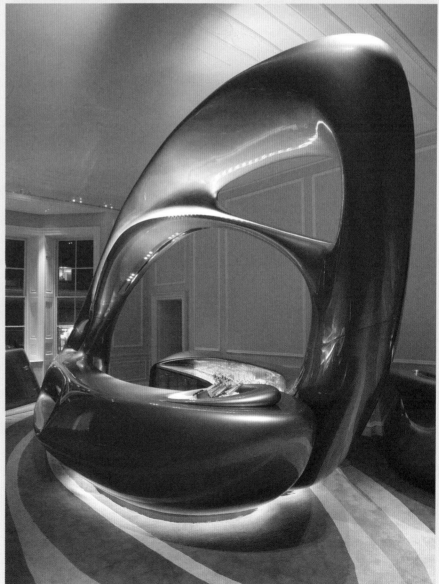

Top
For the bar, the form becomes more complex but its colour complements that of the walls.

Right
Practical components conform to the aesthetic.

Commissioned pieces

Excessive paring away of detail may be the logical conclusion of an objective creative process, but may offer little to which a user can respond emotionally. When a designer is involved in the bigger picture of a complete project, it is often difficult to make the shift in focus necessary to create a piece of furniture with the independent, albeit complementary, presence needed to define the space in which it sits. When such a gesture is called for it may be sensible to recruit a designer or designer/maker, or a team of such to produce the piece or pieces. The interior designer's role is then to orchestrate the communal effort, to select one or more collaborators with compatible aesthetics, and to define and sustain a common aesthetic. To do this successfully is not to lose control but to have the ability to recognize the strengths of others and to assume responsibility for the outcome of the collaboration.

When a designer believes that a particular maker would be best equipped to provide furniture, the client must be persuaded to make the commission. Alternatively the initiative for such an appointment will often come from a client who wants to commission work by the maker of a piece they have already seen and admired.

This news is seldom greeted enthusiastically by a designer, who will inevitably be alarmed about the intrusion of an alien piece into a coherent composition. Either way, the relationship of the designer to the commissioned designer/maker can be delicate and occasionally fraught with a clash of intent and aesthetic. A discussion about the ambition of the project and the context in which it will be deployed will be mutually beneficial, and the earlier the decision is made to commission, the more likely the possibility of a coherent outcome. Predictably, the more experience that the designer/maker has of working to commission, the more likely s/he is to understand the value of creative collaboration. However, ultimately the commissioned designer/maker is being engaged to produce something that is distinctly theirs; this is particularly true when the initiative is the client's. Hence, the designer must be prepared to concede responsibility. If too many stipulations are imposed, then the singular quality the maker has been engaged to provide will be compromised.

Left
Furniture designed for children can be elegant and witty enough to engage the adults obliged to accompany them.

Above
A commissioned curtain of coloured chains divides public areas within a hotel lobby.

Commissioning Traditional Crafts

Crafted pieces have two great strengths. Gifted and experienced makers understand the capacity of their material and respect its limitations as much as they exploit its strengths. With a material as diverse as wood, they will understand the potential of each individual species and of the particularities of each individual piece within that variety. Their work will, however much they strive for perfection, bear the mark of their hand, which is why it is prized and why they must be allowed leeway. It will be cheaper and faster always to use a machine, which will consistently achieve perfection – but will do so without inspiring awe.

Above left and right
Contemporary 'bodging'
'Bodging' is the ironically self-deprecating term employed to describe their craft by those who work with green wood, in the open air or under the simplest self-built shelters, using the most traditional tools and techniques. The term is used wryly because they know that, while they have extraordinary skills, they are at the mercy of the idiosyncrasies of the most disparate of natural materials.

Right
Jointing: holes are chiselled into the seat to receive the verticals that will support the backrest.

Far right
Turning the verticals on a pedal-powered lathe.

Commissioning a Designer / Maker

'Bodgers' (see previous page) are unlikely to make any drawing other than a very perfunctory sketch because they will have a clear idea about the piece they are about to make and will begin to work immediately on the wood, shaping it and, perhaps, modifying their ideas in response to the particular qualities of the raw material.

A designer/maker will, of course, also have a starting point clearly in mind but, because of a pragmatic approach to satisfying what are likely to be more detailed practical requirements, will work with scaled drawings until the form of the end product and the details of its fabrication are wholly resolved. There may be some minor adjustments during the making but essentially

the work will be carried out as in the drawings.

In this example the clients, who were extending and reorganizing a small country house, wanted a new bed with storage in their relocated bedroom. They specified a single structure that would include the bed, drawers, shelves and hanging rails. They also offered a rudimentary plan, which the designer amended after discussion with them and agreement. The major suggested changes were the additions of retractable shelves for books and small personal belongings on each side of the bed and shelves above the bedhead for part of their collection of *objets d'art*. The changes were received enthusiastically.

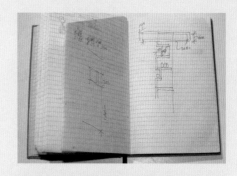

The clients' basic requirements were clear and the designer's speculation was focused on the configuration of the bedhead. The realization that the position of indented shelves should relate to existing niches and the height of these is recorded in a rough sketch.

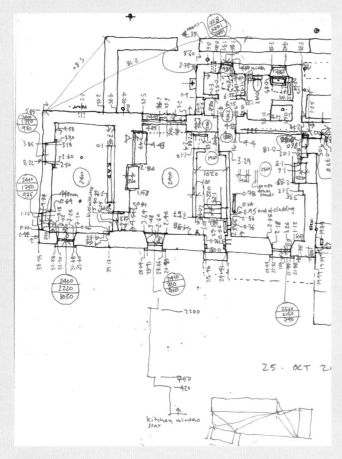

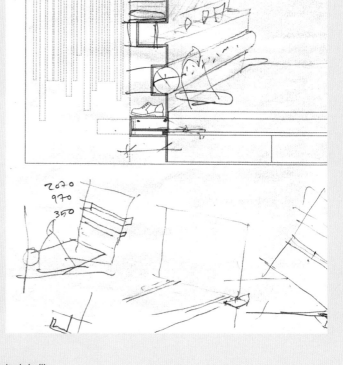

Above
The bed was to be located in the room on the left. The detailed survey of other rooms related to work to be carried out elsewhere in the building.

Above right
A rough measured section is extended with freehand lines, to explain the idea initially to the clients. For clarification, the sketches were made during the meeting with them.

Left
A finalized computer-drawn plan for client approval before making began.
1 Storage area.
2 Hanging rail.
3 Shelves.
4 Retractable shelf.
5 Drawers below bed.
6 Bed.
7 Cover for existing radiator.

Top right
The bed installed.

Middle right
The bedside shelf slides out as required.

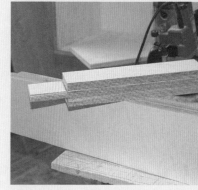

Above
A router makes slots into a plywood sheet to receive the glued edges of components at right angles to it.

Above
Mitred corners are clamped together while the glue sets.

Above
Legs are composites of three glued lengths of plywood, the centre extended to form a 'tenon'.

Left
The 'tenon' slides into the 'mortise' formed by cutting short the centre of the three plywood lengths that make up the edge rail.

PART 3 MATERIALS AND MANUFACTURE

It is often argued that beautiful objects, regardless of the materials and methods used in their production, share the quality of being supremely fit for their purpose. The violin, which might be described as no more than a machine for making music, is cited as an example of a perfect alignment between the aesthetic and the practical, the result of a sustained process of evolution in which every detail – from the pegs for adjusting string tension to the tailpiece over which they are stretched – has been refined until it requires no further amendment and the instrument's form has become synonymous with the sound that it produces. Beauty and practicality have become inseparable. At another extreme, informed opinion has it that the most efficient aeroplanes are the most elegant: their beauty is determined by an inspired response to the laws of aerodynamics, recognition that empathy with the unchangeable forces of nature produces something with which our aesthetic instincts are in tune.

However, no single definitive form for aircraft has evolved and probably never will because of the diversity of specialist functions it must incorporate, all of them further affected by continuous technological advance. Furniture is closer to the aeroplane than the violin in that it caters for a diversity of functions and markets and continues to be subject to developments in material and manufacturing technologies. While the proportions of furniture define its aesthetic credentials, the characteristics that establish its relationship to the time of its creation are found in the details of its construction. The French engineer Auguste Choisy argued in 1899 that shifts in architectural style were dependent on technological advances. The same

may be said about design generally, where the limits of creativity are set by the capacities of materials and of the technologies that shape and connect them.

Every piece of furniture has to stand up to continuous close scrutiny. It has to be practical, easy and comfortable to use, while satisfying the less tangible obligation to satisfy the eye. Practical needs are well defined, comparatively simple to meet and broadly common to all users. There is little hope of concocting pieces that will fundamentally redefine how humans interact with them. The human body and senses evolve too slowly to adopt and adapt to wanton innovation and will not welcome anything that ignores their limitations.

Good furniture is not determined by gratuitous change but by the refinement of archetypes, frequently prompted by the impact of technology on materials and means of production and carried out in response to changes in a wider social context, which is itself increasingly shaped by technological progress. While there is no intrinsic merit in the new and no obligation to reject the past, designers are, and perhaps should be, drawn to the new and, if they are connected to the particularities of their time, their work will reflect it. When Philippe Starck's first chairs appeared they were indisputably, recognizably chairs, but by experimentation with the details of form and materials Starck presented shifts of perception that influenced everything that followed and set standards against which all subsequent work was judged.

Furniture style, whether retrospective or provocatively new, is ultimately determined by detail. Form and materials establish the broad identity but it is in the

Both the piece on this page and that opposite represent how form and a material's physical characteristics are interdependent. The chunky, textured boards and the butted and nailed connections shape the elemental bench **(left)**. The thinking and techniques that underpin it are easily deciphered. In contrast, the freestanding banquette **(right)** is only achievable with steel plate and welded joints. The emphasis is on form and the mechanics of its construction are played down. Welds are ground smooth and the whole is spray-painted to disguise individual components.

nature of the junctions and joints that the aesthetic is definitively expressed. The designer's eye must refine the meeting of verticals and horizontals, the relationship between abutting materials, the connections, whether visible or hidden. Choice of materials will be governed initially by a response to function, of which the obligation to satisfy the human appetite for beauty is a variable component. Materials, whether they perform as finishes or structural components, in turn determine detailing options. Intelligent designers do not force a material to operate beyond its inherent capabilities.

Digital technology has fundamentally affected the way designers work. They have new ways to think, new materials to consider and new ways to turn their thoughts into tangible outcomes. That and concerns about sustainability, the reduction of waste and the conservation of natural resources have changed criteria, and in the immediacy of these fundamental changes it would be easy to forget the designer's obligation to produce objects of aesthetic merit. While a new palette of materials may be replacing some traditional, some less sustainable options, these new and old raw materials together offer as many options as before – probably more – and new methods of making add to the lexicon of viable forms. Traditional joints and jointing strategies,

which are the successful outcomes of protracted trial and error, remain valid, and new machinery can make them faster and more precisely than the best handcrafting. Digital programming facilitates the making of complex forms, for, to the computer, all tasks are equally simple. It is romantic nostalgia and, perhaps, the comparative imperfections, that may commend the handcrafted object. The nature of recent developments, particularly those to do with digital design and digital production, is such that the expression of creativity is freed from human limitations in the making process.

It is technologists who evolve new products and processes but it is designers who must assimilate their potential and their shortfalls and from them create furniture that enhances the lives of its users. Understanding of the practical capabilities of new materials and processes provides the impetus to find the new aesthetic that is inherent within them. To do that convincingly, designers need the appetite to see and engage with possibilities and their experience of established options equips them to speculate successfully about future possibilities.

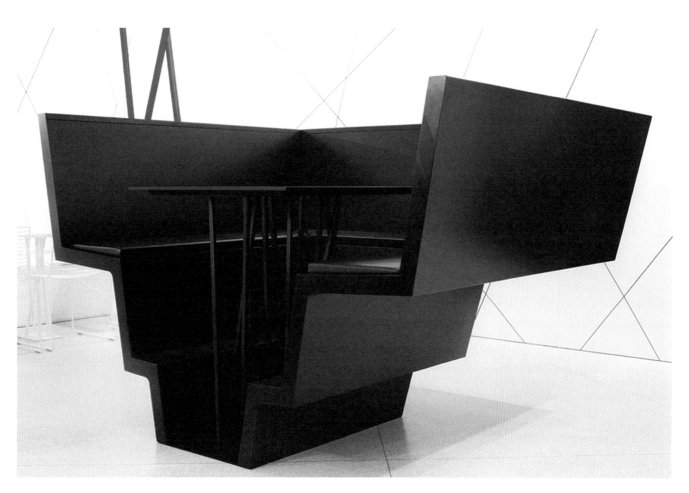

New Techniques, New Aesthetics

Computer Numerical Control

CNC is a generic term for the manufacturing process in which machine tools are programmed and controlled by computer, in effect the digital linking of CAD (computer-aided design) and CAM (computer-aided manufacture). While hand- and machine-making required templates and repetitive production for financial viability, CNC automatically re-programmes to new models without preparation time and without a financial penalty for variations. It is capable of producing pieces of extreme precision and ensures quality control regardless of where it is produced.

Right
A 3-axis CNC router for 2D profiling and 3D prototyping.

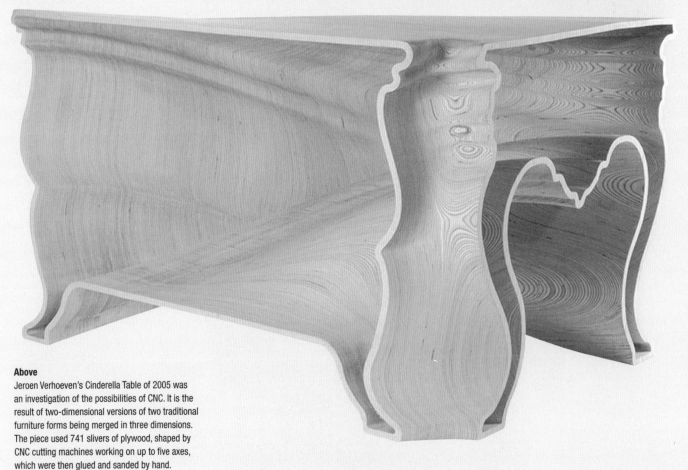

Above
Jeroen Verhoeven's Cinderella Table of 2005 was an investigation of the possibilities of CNC. It is the result of two-dimensional versions of two traditional furniture forms being merged in three dimensions. The piece used 741 slivers of plywood, shaped by CNC cutting machines working on up to five axes, which were then glued and sanded by hand.

Selective laser sintering

SLS is a technique by which an object is built up as layers of powder are laid one on top of the other and a computer-controlled laser beam selectively binds together those particles that will form the three-dimensional section of the proposed object. It enables endless intricate, computer-generated variations of basic forms to be translated into tangible realities.

CNC is probably the most used of the new technologies and has already defined its own aesthetic (see opposite), which would appear to be an obvious exploitation of its potential. Presumably time will lead to the development of more diverse interpretations. SLS has a more limited capacity to turn out large-scale objects but is capable of making much finer and intricate detail. Both make it possible to design anywhere in the world and to have pieces produced anywhere else in the world with a guarantee of the same universal quality.

Right
A light-fitting and a chair produced by SLS techniques.

Materials

Some materials are chosen because of their fitness for practical purposes, others for their aesthetic value, but ideally the selected material will satisfy both criteria since there are few, if any, furniture pieces that a designer creates that do not have a decorative role. Chairs in particular are often treated as decorative objects, traditionally set against a wall and only called occasionally to action. Tables are dedicated to carrying, but when not in use can operate as decorative objects.

Material selection is likely to be as much about tactile qualities as visual ones. Users are more likely to touch furniture, and lifelong experience of touching means most can 'feel' by looking. The following pages list the materials used, to greater or lesser degrees, in furniture making.

Sustainability has become a factor in material selection that cannot, should not, be avoided. The comparatively limited palette of materials suitable for making walls, floors and ceilings means that acceptable materials and construction methods for them are well documented but the much wider range of materials suitable for furniture making means that some product-specific research may be required before a final specification is made purely on aesthetic criteria. Decision-making should not be based solely on the vulnerability of a natural resource but must also take into account the impact of its depletion on the environments of which it is a contributing constituent. Manufacturing processes, their consumption of water and fossil fuels, which are used both in making and transportation, and the waste products that are a legacy of production are also crucial factors in the equation.

The following pages list and describe the materials and related processes used in furniture making.

Right
A newly felled tree. The irregular circumference will be squared before conversion to planks. Waste wood will be converted to timber-based board products such as chipboard and oriented strand board (OSB).

Timber

Timber is the most organic of furniture-making materials, culled directly from a living organism. It is also, probably, the oldest material used by mankind and tried-and-tested techniques have evolved to take advantage of its properties, and to minimize its shortcomings. Its strengths are its appearance and its workability. Its weaknesses are its vulnerability to wet and its tendency, if not properly dried, or 'seasoned', to warp or crack.

There are two categories of timber: hardwood and softwood. Hardwoods and hardwood veneers are almost exclusively used where appearance is the prime consideration. Softwoods are used for hidden framing and elements that are to be painted or normally concealed. The former come from slow-growing trees with closely clustered rings that make a dense, strong wood. They are prized for their rich natural colours and decorative grains. Some of the most exotic and desirable come from endangered and protected species, usually originating in tropical rainforests. Softwoods are fast-growing, essentially a farmed crop. They are therefore easily renewable but make poorer-quality timber. Both types need to be seasoned after felling. Seasoning is the process of allowing the cut wood to lose its natural moisture and sap, to become a stable product that will not shrink or warp. Economic pressures in the softwood markets can lead to poorly seasoned wood, and their more widely spaced growth rings warp more easily.

Planed timbers, often hardwood because of its greater density and greater variety of hues and grain patterns, are normally used as framing members in furniture making and as veneers on plywoods and other composite boards used for panelling and shelving. Composite boards can also serve as framing materials, using specialist jointing devices and techniques. Digitally controlled machinery offers precision-cutting of intricate shapes into and out of sheet materials that may be used to make the complex interlocking forms that bring rigidity and strength to lightweight assemblies.

When a tree is felled, the branches are stripped from its trunk and it is then transported to a sawmill, where the trunk is sawn into planks of varying sizes.

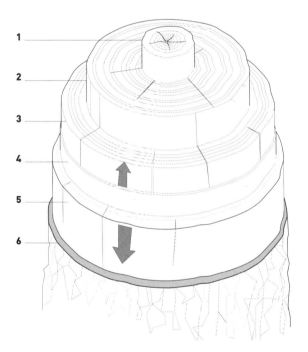

Left
Trunk structure
1   The pith, the remnant of the original shoot.
2   Heartwood, the dead sapwood, formed by the tree adding successive sapwood rings, which deprive the inner sapwood of oxygen and essential nutrients.
3   Sapwood, which carries water to the leaves.
4   Cambium layer, which creates new bast and sapwood.
5   Bast or inner bark, which carries food.
6   Bark, which protects the bast.

Below
Sawn log techniques
Growth rings make wood grain and determine the strength of a piece. There are various ways the trunk may be sawn into planks, to maximize their number.
1   Cross section of a trunk showing annual growth rings.
2   'Plain-sawn', 'flitch-cut' or 'through-and-through' log. Planks cut this way will show the rings running edge to edge.
3   'Quarter-sawn' logs, cut radially from the centre, display the maximum 'figure' or grain pattern and will be harder-wearing.
4   'Radially cut' logs create most waste which can be used in the manufacture of composite boards.

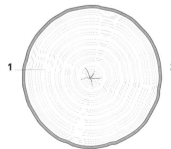
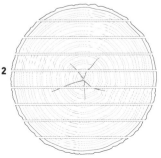
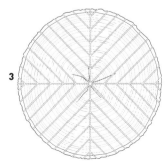
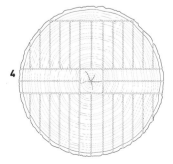

Below

Movement in timbers

1 A log's circumference will decrease as it dries out.
2 A plain-sawn plank will tend to move most across its width and, proportionally, approximately half as much through its thickness.
3 A quarter-sawn plank will have greatest movement in its thickness and will move half as much across its width.
4 The annual rings in a plain-sawn plank vary greatly in length, and as a plank shrinks the wood will pull away from the smallest ring, bending away from what was the heart of the tree.
5 There is virtually no distortion in a quarter-sawn plank.
6 If plants are glued together to create a wider board, setting planks with annual rings alternating will help to keep the board flat.

Timber is generally stable along its length and will not move regardless of humidity, but a log will reduce in circumference during the drying and seasoning process. Poor seasoning will result in warping and bending in timbers and the direction of grain that results from the cutting strategy can exacerbate this movement. While in most instances complete stability will be preferred, it can be useful to exploit the tendencies of certain cuts to distort in particular ways.

Because it is a living organism, when harvested, timber is prone to irregularities and imperfections. Some of these, in some contexts, are seen as positive attributes.

Cutting the trunk to make planks is done on a circular saw and the faces of new planks are rough, torn by the teeth of the saw blade. Softwood is used in this state for structural work, most commonly for floor joists, but all other timber is planed smooth on all sides so that it offers precise surfaces for intricate assembly and finishing. This timber is described as PAR, an abbreviation of 'planed all round'.

Upgrading sawn planks, which are cut to standard dimensions, involves shaving 3mm/$\frac{1}{8}$in off each face so that, for example, a 100 x 50mm/4 x 2in sawn cross section is reduced to 94 x 44mm/3¾ x 1¾in. This will

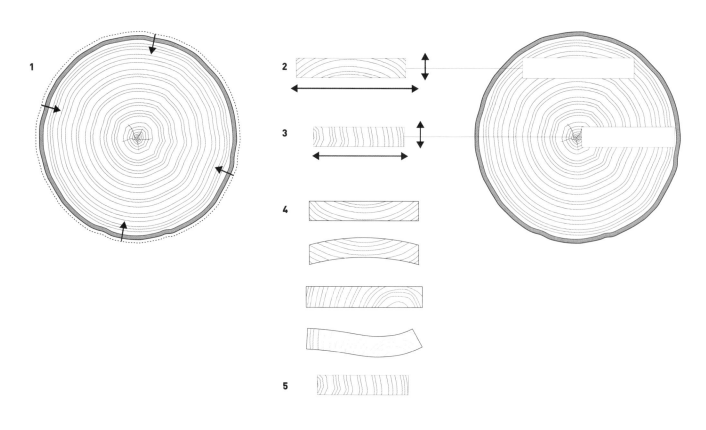

result in a perfectly smooth surface in hardwoods and good-quality softwoods, but poor-quality softwoods will have some surface unevenness, which will be particularly apparent with paint finishes. Blemishes can generally be made good by filling and sanding. Dimensions, after planing, are generally accurate but there can be slight variations in finished sizes. Given the precision of most furniture making, these discrepancies can result in very slight non-alignments which will show in the finished piece, particularly if it is painted with no visible grain to camouflage the joint. It is therefore good practice to create a 'shadow gap' or recess between elements to eliminate direct contact between faces. If they must abut, then post-fixing sanding will create a flush finish. While it is usual to design furniture using standard timber sections, there is no reason why variations cannot be used, particularly with pieces being produced in a workshop.

Below
Irregularities and defects
1 Waney edge, the plank cut from the edge of the trunk. The unevenness of the trunk will result in one uneven edge, which the bast will retain if the bark is stripped off.
2 'End check' can occur because the ends of planks are the first and fastest to dry out.
3 'Live' knots, the ingrowing basal of a cut living branch, may be tacky with resin.
4 'Dead' knots, the dead stump of a broken branch that has been subsumed by the tree. Dead knots will be loose and can fall out.
5 'Cupping', caused during the drying-out process across the width of a plank.
6 'Bowing', caused during the drying-out process along the length of a plank.
7 'Heart and star shakes' develop along the medullary rays, which extend perpendicularly to the growth rings and can embellish the 'figure', or patterning, with, amongst other effects, 'silver grain', 'medullary spots' and 'pith flecks'.
8 'Cup and ring shakes' develop along the lines of annual growth rings and are produced by decay, weathering, felling or badly controlled drying.

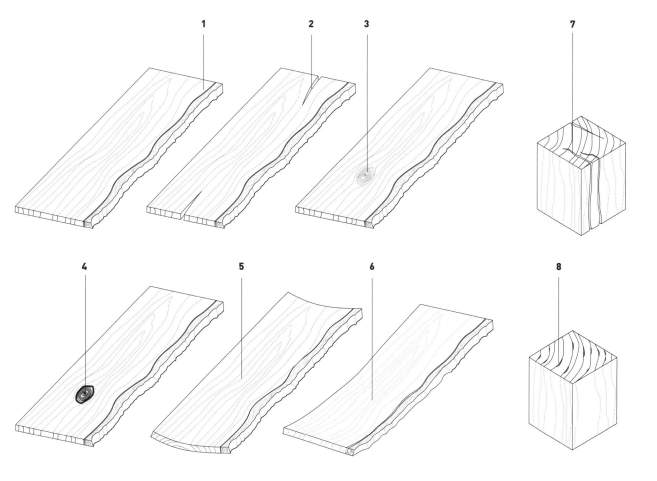

Traditional timber joints

In timber's long history as a furniture-making material, an extensive repertoire of joints has evolved that not only ensure strong, neat junctions but, in some cases, have become decorative elements in their own right, making a virtue of the interaction of smooth, planed surfaces that follow the grain of the wood and the rougher, more open end textured grain. The structure of the joints creates patterns when different grains or timbers are interlocked, and these have become part of the decorative language of furniture design. They help to resolve visually the change of direction at corners.

The joints illustrated are a broad selection of the most common used in solid timber joinery. They illustrate the basic principles of making a sound connection that may be built on in response to particular contexts. While the joints were evolved by and for hand tools, they can all be made by machine, which is faster and therefore cheaper and invariably produces perfect results. Other joints suitable for the more friable cores of timber-based boards, such as MDF and chipboard, which are extensively used in carcassing (concealed framing structures), rely almost exclusively on machine production.

Glue has long been the crucial ingredient in joining timbers. Stronger as a connecting mechanism than screws, much stronger than nails it is, in fact, stronger than the wood itself so that, when an attempt is made to pull a joint apart, the glued interface will remain intact and the wood will splinter at its weakest point.

Traditional wooden joints maximize the surface area to which glue may be applied, integrating areas of cohesion into the core of each component of the joint. A well-made joint also ensured and ensures perfect alignment, or deliberate misalignment, of the faces of each component. The visible evidence of jointing has become a familiar element in pieces of furniture, visible expressions of the mechanics of junctions.

Furniture joints

1	Finger or comb.	**8**	Biscuit.
2	Through dovetail.	**9**	Wedged tenon.
3	Half-blind dovetail.	**10**	Haunched tenon.
4	Sliding dovetail.	**11**	Stub tenon.
5	Housing.	**12**	Foxtail wedged tenon.
6	Mortise and tenon.	**13**	Bridle.
7	Dowelling.	**14**	Halving.
		15	Mitre halving.
		16	Mitre dowelling.
		17	Dovetail bridle.
		18	Butt.

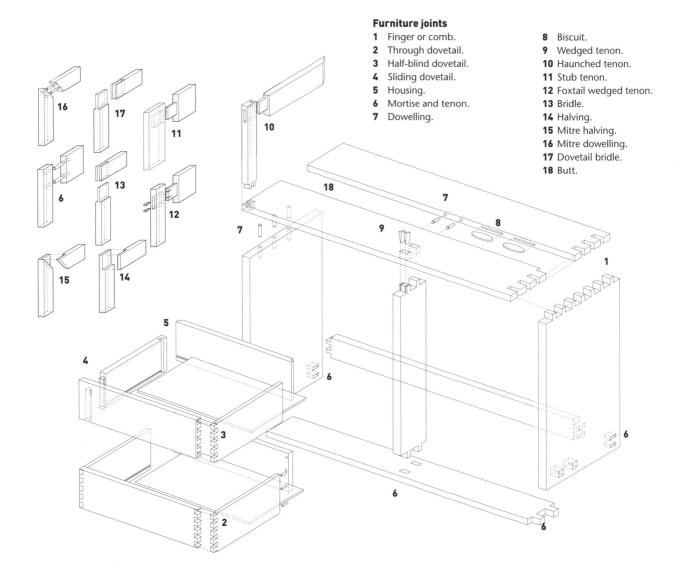

Experimental timber joints

All the illustrated joints respond to new materials and technologies. They are singular reinterpretations of how a chair might be constructed but all respect the ergonomic obligations that shape every chair. They also underline the truism that decoration is most appropriately located at significant points, such as junctions of elements or materials. While they do not conform to familiar perceptions of decoration, they define and enhance the object of which they are a part. All are necessarily experimental; further development of each will either refine it or demonstrate that it lacks the capacity to match tried-and-tested technologies.

A The jointing pieces are made from polycaprolactone wax, which can be softened in an oven or in hot water. Colour pigments may be added to the melted wax to give it colour. Once soft, it can be modelled by hand and allowed to cool and harden to make the connection. The wax works best when applied to a rough or roughened surface. Holes can be drilled into the wood to increase grip. Forming the joint is necessarily an intuitive process but understanding of how to thicken the wax at crucial points improves with experience. Adjustments can be made after initial hardening if the wax is softened with a heat gun. In this prototype the joints are crude in deliberate contrast to the precision of the timber but obviously they can be worked to a more refined conclusion. The wax can also be smeared thinly, dripped to form a decorative skin or poured into a mould and allowed to set.

B Another example of a plastic joint, in this case polyurethane foam, connecting timber components.

C Each timber element is broken and the ragged ends provide a key and, because the breaking is uncontrolled, each joint is unlike any other.

D The timbers are placed in a mould and when the foam is added, it insinuates itself into the ragged, broken ends.

E Jointing units are made from recycled paper and textiles and renewable sources of cellulose like hemp and bamboo. It is 95 per cent water when first applied and shrinks as it dries, shrinks to grip the timbers.

F The 'elastic' components, here coloured pink, are inserted in the wooden frame and, while naturally assuming the curve defined by the rigid timber members, allow the frame to flex.

G Counterintuitively, the smooth wood is contrasted with the rough texture of the joints, perhaps signalling that the material is recycled.

H Joints are made from a material based on cellulose fibres.

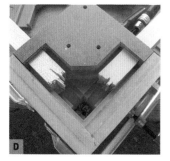

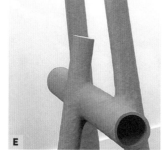

Exploring Potential
Shrink Series – Nicola Zocca

This proposal uses a kind of tape normally employed to protect electrical cables and engineering parts. When heated using hot air, it shrinks to between a third and a sixth of its diameter and grips hard enough to form a permanent connection.

Right
A complicated joint may be strengthened with some simple machining. The nature of the tube's application can cope with minor inaccuracies.

The seat and back are powder-coated steel. The legs and seat support are of timber.

Holes cut in the steel tabletop help lock the angles of the legs.

Joints are visually consistent.

Marquetry

Marquetry, the craft of applying thin veneers to a base structure, is a technique for creating representational or abstract surface patterns. The decorated surface is two-dimensional but the pattern frequently suggests a third dimension. Veneers are usually wood, chosen for their colour, but metals, bone, shell or any other material that can be sliced thin enough and is robust enough to withstand the anticipated wear may be used.

Parquetry uses the same techniques and materials but the term refers specifically to the making of repeating geometric patterns. Inlay refers to the cutting out of one solid material, usually wood, to receive another solid piece of precisely the same shape but different colour or texture.

Left
Pieces were made using laser-cut stainless-steel templates.

Below
Some of the traditional taste for optical illusion is exploited in this contemporary example, where veneers appear to be wrapped over the angle of top and side, suggesting solid, three-dimensional elements, while, paradoxically, chamfered edges to top and side reduce the perceived bulk.

Exploiting Potential
'Burr Elm' Table – Danny Lane

The burr condition is caused by a growth on an elm tree trunk that results in a particularly exotic, swirling grain. It is popular for decorative woodwork.

Below
The top is formed from two lengths of wood that are taken from the same area of the tree and, when brought together so that each mirrors the other, form a tabletop with a central, broadly symmetrical void. The edges of the timber top are naturally ragged; this is echoed in the stacked glass legs. Glued horizontal laminations of glass are the designer's trademark.

Bottom
Steel rods that pass through the centre of the legs connect to the steel frame.

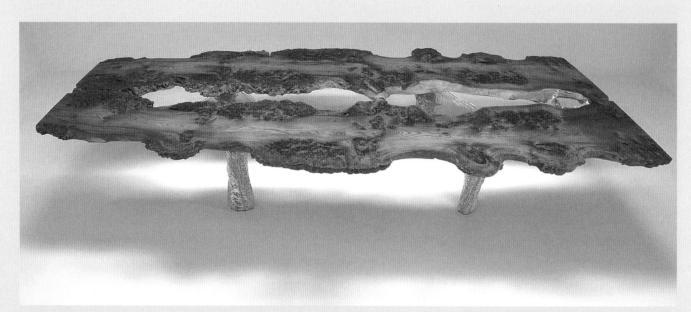

Above
The irregularly shaped pieces of stacked glass have an affinity with the grain of the wood. The five top laminations, when glued together, are strong enough to give stability.

Left
Surface grain and cross section are both richly distorted.

Timber-based boards

Unless they are substantial enough to be converted into smaller planks or strips, branches stripped from tree trunks and other waste material from the sawmilling process are converted into the strands and fibres that are, in turn, processed into various composite boards, such as blockboard, chipboard, medium-density fibreboard (MDF) and oriented strand board (OSB). They tend to be used for carcassing. The first three can also be finished with timber, plastic, metal or paper laminates; their cross-grained structure makes them particularly stable.

Timber veneers, which are 0.6mm-/less than $^1/_{16}$in-thick sheets of timbers selected for their decorative grain and colour, are used extensively in furniture making to provide a natural wood finish over a large planar area. Logs are immersed in boiling water or steam to soften them. Bark is removed and the logs are mechanically shaved to produce a continuous, thin sheet that is glued to a backing board for strength and stability.

The number of appropriate sheet materials is constantly expanding, especially as concerns for sustainability increasingly influence selection. Reconstituted bamboo, which is a particularly fast-growing wood, and recycled plastics and paper products represent the vanguard of the exploitation of materials that were formerly treated as waste. Specialist websites provide information about innovations and more conventional materials. If a material appears promising it is a simple matter to request a sample online and ask specific questions about its performance.

Making veneers
Rotary-cutting: logs, stripped of their bark, are cut to match the length of the cutting blade and rotated on a lathe. A cutting edge parallel to the lathe first makes a smooth cylinder and is then reset to slice off a thin continuous sheet of veneer, which is trimmed, dried and graded. Rotary-cut veneers are mostly used for plywood manufacture.

Below
Slicing produces a more decorative veneer. Logs are set vertically and moved up and down against a diagonal blade. The best veneers are taken from the centre of the log. Better-quality decorative veneers are made by slicing quarter-sawn sections of log.

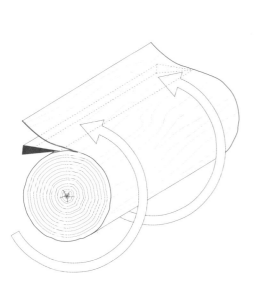
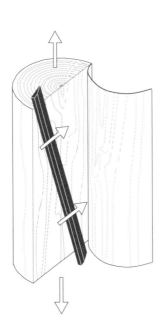
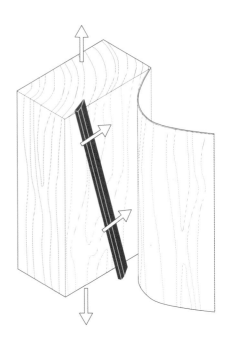

Plywood

More than the other timber-based boards, plywood retains the grains and colours of the natural wood. It consists of thin layers, or veneers, of timber glued together, with the grain of each running at right angles to those next to it. This cross-grained sandwiching neutralizes the tendency of the board to warp in damp conditions to create a very stable material.

Plywood is graded for performance and quality of surface veneer. The thinner the individual veneers, the better the board. Cheaper boards have little graining and thick core layers and are primarily used for carcassing. Good-quality plywood has thin, dense veneers and its edges have a sharp, linear pattern, good enough to be exposed as a finished decorative edge.

The boards are relatively easily cut, although the cut edges of the cheaper products may fray. When plywood is used as a finished surface the staining necessary to protect it will enhance its grain. Dyes can add coloured tints and even a clear protective stain will darken its natural colour.

Below
Plywood is versatile, equally effective for freestanding pieces, fixed shelving, and cladding. Together they become more than the sum of their parts.

Below right
The laminations on the exposed edges of good-quality plywood offer a decorative possibility. Mitred joints allow lamination lines to turn corners.

MDF

Medium-density fibreboard (MDF) is made from wood fibres glued together under heat and pressure. It comes in various thicknesses, from 3 to 30mm/¼ to 1¼in, is very stable, and has hard and very smooth faces. When spray-painted, its appearance is identical to that of painted metal.

The material has no true grain and can therefore be machined with great accuracy and without surface damage. This simplifies the cutting of sharp, precise angles, particularly useful in the making of seamless mitred corners, which gives it considerable advantages over other timber-based boards but its density makes it the heaviest and its raw edges can crumble under impact.

While the faces of MDF boards provide an excellent base for paint finishes, the softer, mushier core, which is exposed on all edges, is more absorbent and, if exposed, should be treated with filler or sealer to provide a non-porous core for painting that will ensure a tone and reflectivity consistent with the primary faces. While the material does not have a strong grain, a clear sealant will bring out a rich ginger tone with a slight fleck patterning. It provides a stable base for veneer and laminates. Some manufacturers make coloured boards that are pigmented through their core. Others produce thin boards with grooves cut in one face so that they bend easily and evenly.

The material contains urea formaldehyde, which is released particularly during cutting and sanding and can damage eyes and lungs. Standard workshop precautions will eliminate dangers but care should be taken with on-site work. The chemical will continue to be released gradually throughout the life of the product so a paint or sealant finish is necessary to contain it.

The wood workshop

A professional wood workshop contains a battery of heavy-duty cutting, drilling and sanding machines, which ensure perfect alignment and dimensional control.

A Sliding support beds and rollers allow board materials to be fed evenly and precisely onto the blade of a circular saw.

B Curved profiles are cut by manoeuvring sheet materials against the thin, vertical blade of a jigsaw as they are pushed across the fixed, horizontal bed.

C A portable circular saw, the blade can be adjusted and locked in the vertical and horizontal planes for cutting angles and mitres.

D A rotating sander smooths ends.

E A fixed, vertical stand ensures drilling at exactly 90 degrees to the horizontal and control over drilling depth.

Woodworking lathe

Lathes are used to convert lengths of square-sectioned material into cylinders. Identical in principle to the foot-operated lathe of the traditional 'bodger', the power-driven lathe operates by revolving a length of wood at great speed against an abrasive edge to make a circular section and modifications to the diameter of the section at points along its length create an undulating profile.

Top
Some of the bulk of the original length is planed off to speed up the process.

Middle
The length of wood is held firmly between adjustable clamps and rotated at speed to create a cylindrical cross section.

Bottom
A hand-held chisel, braced against the body of the lathe, cuts evenly and precisely into the cylindrical section. Guidelines are marked in pencil.

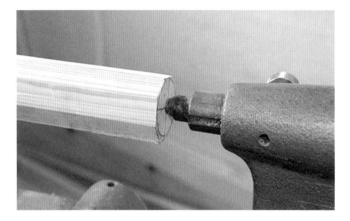

The Versatility of Wood
Private Club – LWD

As a natural material wood is, with very few exceptions, a reassuringly renewable source. It offers very generous options to the furniture designer, not only with its range of hues and grains but also in the way it may be treated and finished. These furniture pieces, designed as one-off pieces for a private club, demonstrate its versatility.

The squares of end-grain wood, glued to a plywood base board, that make up the top of the communal dining table create a mosaic of varied colour and texture. Wood types may be mixed for greater visual definition but even when only one species is used the variation in adjacent pieces will be clear. Since the more open texture of end grain is more absorbent, sealing the wood is important, particularly for a dining table, which will be frequently cleaned and exposed to food and liquids.

On the long bench, bark is left on the sides and feet of an unbroken length of tree trunk, which is used almost as it left the sawmill. Only the sitting surface is planed smooth but the crack in the surface is accepted happily as further evidence of the raw material. Top, sides and feet are sealed to enhance colour and grain and to make cleaning easier, particularly in the case of the bark.

Left
End-grain squares, glued to a plywood base board, provide both regular and irregular patterning.

Above
The sawn, sanded and sealed tree trunk provides a muscular contrast to the otherwise refined furniture. It defines territories within the bigger space, representing a very minimal, very deliberate working of the basic material.

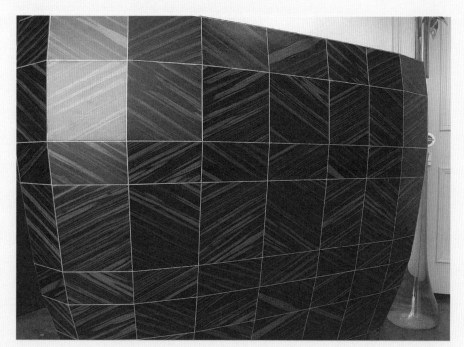

Left
The plywood substructure of the reception desk is clad in a mosaic of African tulip-wood tiles. The high-gloss varnish emphasizes the play of light on the faceted surface.

Below
Reception desk: plan and elevations.
3mm/¼in 'tiles' of gloss-sealed African tulip-wood clad the birch plywood subframe of the reception desk.

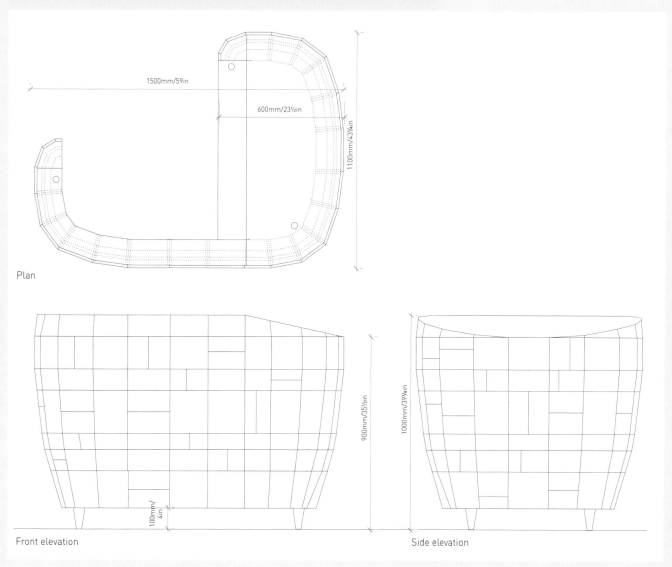

1500mm/59in

600mm/23½in

1100mm/43¾in

Plan

900mm/35½in

1000mm/39¾in

100mm/4in

Front elevation

Side elevation

Metals

In furniture design, metals may be purely utilitarian or purely decorative but usually they are a combination of both. Examples of the utilitarian are mild steel and aluminium, of the decorative, stainless steel and brass, silver and gold. Some, such as zinc, copper and titanium, have specific practical applications in the building industry but, like all others, may be used as applied finishes. Steel and aluminium tubes are widely used for structural framing, both exposed and concealed, and their natural finish can be upgraded. Steel may be chromed and aluminium-coloured. Significant sustainability concerns, primarily relating to mining and manufacturing processes, attach to all of them.

Metal hollow tubes and solid bars are stronger than the same section in timber. Tubes have greater resistance to bending than bars and reduce weight. Both allow structures that are more visually delicate but which, with welded, screwed or bolted joints, have great rigidity and strength. Welded joints are initially crude and, while acceptable for hidden joints, will need to be ground smooth if they are exposed. There is a wide range of metal screws and bolts capable of comparable performance, and selection depends on the preferred visual detail. A length

of jointing tube, with an outer diameter equal to the inner diameter of the framing tube, inserted into the junction of two butting pieces will give rigidity to the joint. Thin metal sheet, usually steel or aluminium, may be folded, with either right-angled or radiused bends for strength and rigidity. If quarter-circle curved edges, which strengthen and stiffen thin metal shelves, have the same inner radius as the tubular frame that supports them, they will drop precisely and securely into place.

Metals may be used with their natural finish. Of those that do, the most common are mild steel, which may be spray-painted to prevent rust, stainless steel, which requires no protection, and aluminium, which may also be colour-coated. More expensive options are brass, copper, chrome and an extensive range of chemically induced coloured patinations. Metal frames are often used with glass for display cabinets, with the glossy and reflective finishes of stainless steel or chrome favoured as more visually compatible with glass.

A A length of tube inserted into each end of abutting tubes and locked in position with set screws will ensure a rigid junction.

B, C & D Joints may also be made by cutting male and female threads into abutting lengths of tube and screwing them together.

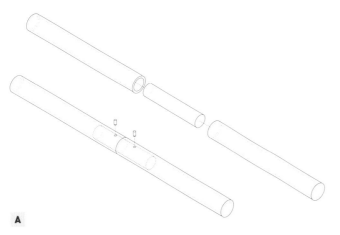

A

B

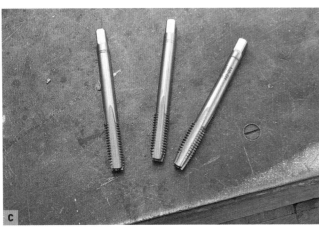

C

D

Below
Steel sheet, with welded joints, allows familiar café elements to be interpreted with diagrammatic simplicity.

Left
Folded, perforated aluminium sheet unifies walls and reception desk.

Above
Magnetic discs placed in the toes of shoes clamp them securely on top of stainless-steel display posts.

Steel

There are two types. Mild steel, which in its natural state is a flat grey colour, is available in a range of hot- and cold-rolled sections, which improve its basic structural capability. They may be welded or bolted together. The latter technique, in which holes for bolts can be pre-drilled before the sections are brought to site, while not as strong as welding, allows for some adjustment on site. It must be painted or oiled to prevent rust.

Stainless steel, which is an alloy with a minimum of 10 per cent chromium content, has a highly reflective finish and is resistant to rust but can still suffer corrosion.

Painting provides the simplest method of protecting steel but other, more complex options, particularly galvanizing with a film of zinc or other reactive coatings, offer more permanent protection. Chrome-plating of mild steel provides a corrosion-resistant, highly reflective finish.

Aluminium

About one-third the weight of steel, aluminium is naturally protected from corrosion by a thin layer of aluminium oxide that forms on its surface when it is exposed to air. It can be extruded into sections similar to those for steel or rolled to make thin laminates that may be glued to timber composite boards. It is easily shaped by a cold-pressing process, and thin sheets may be folded to stiffen and strengthen them.

In its natural state aluminium looks similar to mild steel but can be coloured, most effectively by a powder-coating process in which powdered pigment is applied electrostatically and heat-cured to create an even skin that is tougher than conventional paints.

While its mining and initial production processes are considered ecologically unsound, aluminium has the virtue of being easy and cheap to recycle, requiring only 5 per cent of the energy needed to process raw natural ore. Recycled material, described as 'secondary aluminium', is used extensively in the production of extrusions.

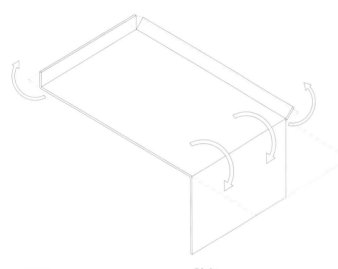

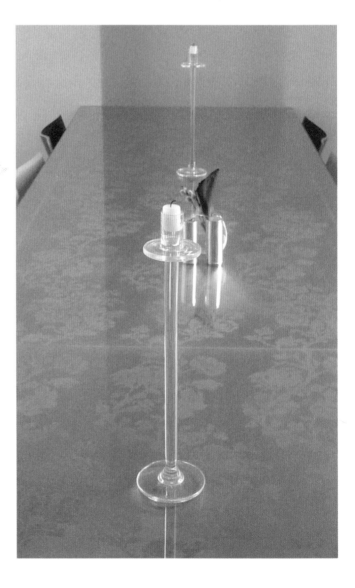

Above
Folding, bending and corrugating add rigidity and strength to thin metal sheets.

Right
Etched metal: for this table top a pattern, derived from a textile was acid-etched into four pieces of mild steel. A single sheet of glass was laid on top to protect the pattern and facilitate cleaning.

A metal workshop

The various metals used in furniture making are at least as versatile as wood but are significantly more difficult to work. Processes involving heat and heavy machinery are not feasible for work on site and fabrication is carried out in specialist workshops of varying sizes with different degrees of expertise – comparatively small and comparatively few items may be handled along with more substantial commissions.

Metals may be worked with great precision and computer-controlled machinery is making complex operations simpler. Bespoke pieces become more practical and economical but, as always, discussion with specialists will refine ideas and, frequently, point to new directions.

A A typical metal workshop with specialist machinery, gas containers to power welding tools and racks for the storage of sheet metal and extrusions.

B Many technical processes are now programmed by computer.

C Welding is a generic name for a range of techniques that use heat to fuse sections of steel together. It is used across a spectrum of connections, from major structural members to the creation of delicate decoration.

D After welding, it may be necessary, particularly for delicate components, to grind off the uneven lumps of melted metal.

E Plasma-cutting using a 'plasma torch' involves an inert gas being blown at high speed while an electric arc turns it to 'plasma', hot enough to melt metal and blow molten material away from the cut.

F A metalwork lathe operates on the same principles as a timber lathe but, because of the greater force required to work the material, cutting is done by high-strength metal points integral to the lathe.

Traditional metal production: forging

Steel and other metals can be heated in a forge until malleable and then shaped by hammering and twisting. In skilled hands the techniques are suited to producing large-scale but refined and unique components. No piece will exactly replicate another because of the volatility of what is essentially a violent process. The inevitable irregularities are one of the reasons for specifying the technique.

A & B Red-hot metal is malleable and can be formed with a hammer or bent to shape.

C Two convoluted pieces, which each began as straight rods, are bolted together at their shared centre.

D Even when, at first sight, the two halves may seem symmetrical, the technique introduces irregularities.

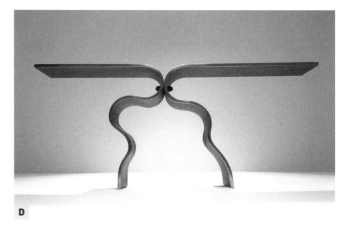

Digital metal production

The compatibility of design software packages and digitally controlled machinery has prompted very significant speculation about new forms and production methods that are changing not just the way that metal furniture is made but the way it looks. Particularly interesting are the possibilities for small production runs, made specifically to order, that are no more expensive per unit (and perhaps cheaper) when made using CNC machinery, or computer-controlled manufacture, than mass-produced options. The variations being generated by new technologies offer further confirmation of Choisy's contention that style evolves from, and is defined by, technological innovations. It does, however, require designers' imaginations to recognize and realize their potential.

Angles Add Rigidity
Folded Furniture Series – The Bakery

A flat, thin sheet of metal may be easily bent and will have little load-bearing strength. Bending along an edge, or creating corrugations over the whole area will add depth and resistance to bending and therefore strength. This furniture range exploits that characteristic to produce pieces that are extremely light but capable of matching the performance of conventional metal or wooden options. Perforations are punched into the metal along predetemined fold lines which make them comparatively weaker at those places and easier to fold with precision.

Below
Stacking stools: the bending and creasing strengthens the thin metal.

Bottom left
Stacking chairs: the width of material at the junction of seat and back provides stiffness.

Bottom right
The folding techniques used to make paper models were an accurate reflection of those used in the final production.

Plastics

The extensive range of products collected under the generic heading of plastics, each the outcome of different chemical and production processes, are among the materials most maligned for their poor environmental credentials. The gravest offenders are those produced from oil-based sources and those that are not biodegradable. If these objections are ignored, the material has many advantages. Some types are easily moulded, some have great strength-to-weight and -volume ratios, some have great resistance to corrosion, some are highly hygienic. They can be used as resilient decorative and practical finishes or concealed as pipework and conduits with inclusive connective devices that take advantage of the material's suitability for delicate moulding. They are useful substitutes for natural materials. Some are as hard as stone without its permeability and easier to shape in moulds. Virtuous options that overcome ethical objections are increasingly appearing. Bio-based plastics are made from plant sources rather than oil derivatives, although the impact of these new crops on their immediate environment and food production also causes concerns. Recycled plastics are made from reconstituted

waste materials, although not all plastics are suitable for the processes involved but many offer unfamiliar and creatively stimulating ranges of colours, integral patterns and textures. Production of recycled plastics is increasing and, while ranges and structural potential are limited, the market for innovative finishes, boosted by sustainability legislation that encourages recycling, will drive development. Presently properties are generally poor, although tubes, corrugated and honeycomb sheets have some rigidity.

Plastics are extensively used as laminates, which are available in very comprehensive ranges of both flat colours and patterns. Digital printing has made the manufacture of small runs of bespoke patterned sheets much more practical and financially viable. One problem with any laminate-covered sheet materials in furniture-making is that, when cut, the core of the sheet is exposed. To counteract this, edges may be finished either at the point of manufacture or during fabrication with thin 'lipping' strips glued to the exposed edges of the board. More expensive materials are available that have a coloured core which matches the exposed faces.

Left and bottom left
Seating, in a hotel's event room, may be set out conventionally for conferences or stacked away to form a decorative wall. The resilient foam core of each piece compensates for the anthropometric compromises necessary for interlocking storage.

Below
Plastics are particularly versatile. In this restaurant fibreglass cladding panels make a translucent screen that sits comfortably with plastic chairs and corrugated ceiling panels.

Acrylic

Acrylic is the most common of the transparent, translucent and opaque plastic sheets that offer a practical and economic alternative to specialist glasses. While trade names, such as Perspex and Plexiglas, are familiar, it is better to use the generic label since all similar products are derived from acrylic acid.

There are two methods of manufacture. Extruded or continuous cast production is cheaper but the material is softer, more easily scratched and contains impurities that affect its strength. Product made by the cell cast method is superior. The standard sheet can be coloured with the addition of dyes during manufacture.

Acrylic has a number of advantages over glass. Its transparency makes it the clearest material and it remains clear regardless of its thickness, while glass develops a green tint as it gets thicker. Nor does it turn yellow, become brittle or fracture with age. It is significantly stronger than unreinforced glass and half its weight. It is easier to work with. It will not shatter but breaks into large pieces without sharp edges. It can be cut with a saw, is better for making acute internal corners and can be drilled to receive screws. It is easy to bend and therefore better than glass for making two-dimensional curves. Although

more easily scratched than glass, polishing or heating the surface will remove blemishes. It can be easily shaped and joined by heat or solvents. It dissolves, fuses and sets, making an almost invisible weld. Corners cannot be mitred but light is refracted through glued butt junctions with a particular intensity.

Acrylic is particularly useful for display and exhibition cabinets. It has low reflectivity and its inherent strength and flexibility copes well with viewers leaning on it. Its resistance to impact also makes it more secure than cheaper types of glass. There are a number of acrylic-based, solid-coloured core sheet materials that, because of their dense, non-porous structure, are frequently used as worktops in kitchens, bars and laboratories. One of the great advantages they offer is that they can be shaped and moulded so that drainage slots and sinks can be integral to the worktop. Their malleability and versatility make them useful across a greater spectrum of applications and contexts. Only comparatively high cost prevents their wider use. Joins can be rendered invisible and blemishes repaired using the techniques for mending clear acrylic.

Below
A pattern is cut into but not through the solid-coloured bar top and the light source under it shines through the thinner material of the incised pattern.

Right
Acrylic panels, fixed to floor, wall and ceiling, define booths and increase privacy.

The Versatility of Acrylic
A Poet's Chair – LWD

This ceremonial chair, which pivots open to become a lectern, is an excellent example of how form need not timidly follow function but can be prompted by it and by an intention to make a beautiful and expressive resolution of prosaic practicalities.

The particular capacities of acrylic, its lightness when compared to glass, which is important with an interactive piece of furniture, the comparative ease with which it may be cut and etched and, crucially, its response to light, are fundamental to the piece's evolution.

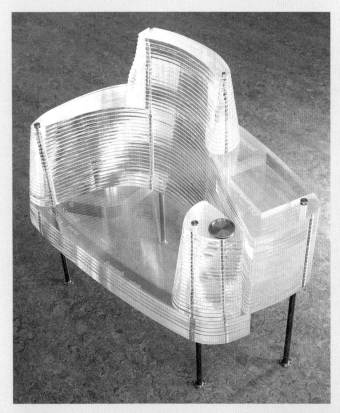

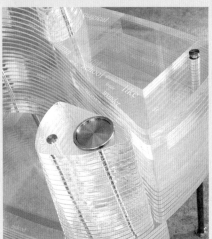

Above left and right
The chair is made of layers of CNC laser-cut 12mm/½in acrylic. The edges were 'flame-polished' with a blowtorch, which makes them completely clear.

Far left
Layers are connected by metal rods/legs that pass through holes in each layer.

Left
The material lends itself easily to intricate etching.

Glass

'Clear float' glass is free of distortion and excessive reflection and has replaced 'plate' and 'sheet' glass, although the former term is still used to describe high-quality glass and the latter to describe thin sheets. In manufacture, molten glass, of which the main ingredient is quartz sand, or 'silica', is poured over a bed of tin and then hardened (or annealed) by controlled cooling. Thicknesses range from 2 to 25mm/^{1}/$_{16}$ to 1in, with sheet sizes of up to 3180 x 4600mm/125¼ x 181in. It is unlikely that very large sheets will be used in furniture but it is always worth checking that those specified can be manoeuvred through openings and around corners on site. It is possible, but difficult, to curve glass by heating a flat sheet over a metal mould or 'refractory'.

Different qualities of glass are produced using a range of techniques that determine strength and appearance. They can have varying degrees of transparency and translucency. They can be coloured and textured. When used in furniture, they can be set within a timber or metal frame, but toughened or laminated glass is sufficiently strong and rigid to act as a table or counter surface without framing. When used without framing, glass edges should be ground smooth for safety.

Grey, green and bronze colours can be created by variations in the proportion of ingredients, which results in selective absorption of parts of the light spectrum. However, since changing the proportions of a mix is a lengthy operation, modifications to basic clear glass are usually made by surface coatings applied during manufacture ('on line') or after ('off line').

Types of glass

Toughened glass is made by heating and rapid cooling the basic material produced in the primary manufacturing process. It is four times stronger and better able to deal with impact, loading or impact stresses. When broken, it disintegrates into small, smooth-edged fragments, which makes it safer. It cannot be cut or worked after manufacture; modifications will cause it to fracture. Edges must be ground smooth before the toughening process. Holes for fixings may be drilled but their size and position are limited. A variety of types of glass, including tinted, patterned and reflective, can be toughened.

Laminated glass consists of sheets bonded to a clear plastic core, to which the glass adheres when broken, which provides a safety factor. Varying thicknesses of the plastic layer can provide protection against hammers, bullets and bombs. Sheet sizes can be up to 5000 x 2500mm/196¾ x 98½in. Patterns can be printed onto the inner faces of the glass, which protects them from abrasion.

Sandblasted glass is made by pitting the surface with sand propelled under high pressure. Areas can be masked off to create varying degrees of pitting for tonal patterns or to leave transparent areas. The process is difficult to control and fine detail should be avoided. Staining of the blasted sections, particularly by the natural oils on hands, can be a problem. Protective coatings have been developed but consideration of where the glass will be used is important.

Acid-etching allows greater control than sandblasting and is better suited to making fine detail. Controlled

Left
Resin-bonded recycled glass may be used in bar tops, worktops and tables. After casting, it is ground smooth to make a highly reflective and intensely patterned surface.

Below left
The material can be moulded to meet practical requirements.

Right
Mirrored glass blocks, with glued joints, both disappear and deceive.

erosion of the surface with hydrofluoric acid will produce varying degrees of translucency.

'Brilliant' cutting, when patterns are incised into the thickness of the glass and edges are smoothed and polished, catches and exploits light.

Opal glass is available in various colours and forms, ranging from a translucent white, or 'flashed opal', to opaque, or 'pot opal'.

Glass has considerable strength in both compression and tension and may be used to stiffen the frameworks that support it. It may be drilled to receive screws and bolt fixings. Specialist adhesives now make the butt-jointing of sheets feasible and reliable and three-dimensional grid constructions can be designed to be self-supporting. Such constructions can offer complete transparency, with minimal distortion. Where a greater degree of visual separation is required in a divider, translucent or opaque glasses may be used and there are interesting possibilities offered by a combination of two, with clear as a possible third component.

Cutting and shaping

Simple, straight lines may be cut by traditional scoring and snapping techniques. Curves and irregular shapes will require a template to guide the cutting tool. Acute internal corners are points of weakness; if used, the corner should be rounded to eliminate the concentration of stress that will occur at the junction of the two straight lines. The centre of drilled holes should be located a minimum of four times the thickness of the glass from its edge. New techniques, using laser and high-pressure water jets, have opened up options for curves and angles.

Joining glass

In traditional furniture making glass was used in small pieces, because of the fragility that then characterized it, and it was almost invariably held in wooden frames, like small windows. It was certainly never used as a load-bearing component or in vulnerable locations. Significant technical advances in the recent past, made both to the inherent strength of the material and the techniques for working it, have significantly added to the range of its potential applications.

Even in its traditional forms thick glass has very considerable strength and may be used for decorative furniture pieces. Mechanical connections may be made with bolts passed through pre-drilled holes in components. It is good practice to place a rubber or neoprene washer between nuts and glass to prevent cracking, either due to excessive tightening or the flexing of components during use.

There have been significant technical advances made in the recent past to both the performance of glass and the techniques for working it. Most of the spectacular innovation in glass production has related to its environmental performance as a collector and conserver of solar energy, and is unlikely to be relevant to furniture design; the potential for cutting more complex shapes than with traditional techniques, however, offers interesting possibilities. Specialist glues have made butt-jointing possible without any mechanical connections; such joints are 'invisible' and extremely strong.

Left
Glass is an appropriate material for the reception desk/ bar in a jeweller's shop.

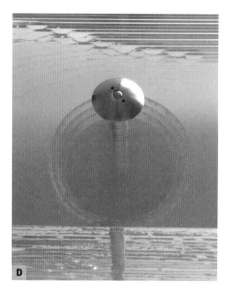

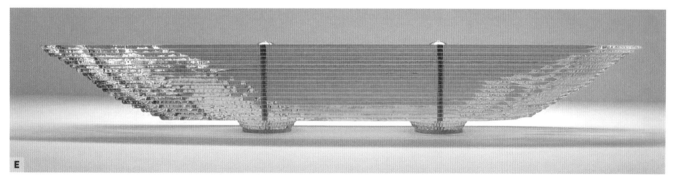

A Etruscan Chair. Glass slabs for the seat and back are strong enough to resist the pivotal forces at the connection points with the steel components. They are not designed for comfort, however.

B & C Greenstone Table (B), Emerald Table (C). Different edge conditions affect response to light.

D 'Hiawatha' Bench. Layers of glass are clamped together and the uneven edge and angled 'prows' accentuate the light.

E 'Hiawatha' Bench. The rods are tightened to clamp the sheets of glass together and disappear into the receding circles cut in each layer to receive them.

All pieces on this page by Danny Lane.

Adapting Techniques
Blown-glass Chair – Heatherwick Studio

This experiment demonstrates that even the most traditional techniques, in glass or any other material, may be adapted to create radically unfamiliar forms in furniture making.

The outcome of glass blowing relies heavily on the spontaneous response of the blower to the evolving nature of the object during the production process. While skilled glass blowers have great control over the end result, they do not, and could not, work precisely to dimensioned drawings. A designer can provide little more than conceptual sketches and hope to evolve a shared perception of the desired outcome with the makers. With a chair such as this the likelihood of its conforming to recognized anthropometric standards is very slight and its role will be primarily decorative, and provocative.

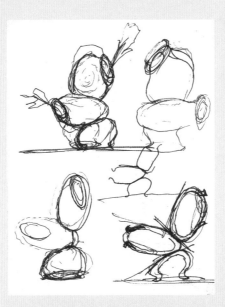

Left
Speculative sketches form the basis for discussion between designer and maker. The definitive form can only emerge during the very volatile making process.

Below left
Both material and technique are untried in furniture making and the result is a radically unfamiliar form.

Below
While the glass blower will have the image in mind, the making process relies on intuitive judgement and spontaneous response to the behaviour of the molten material.

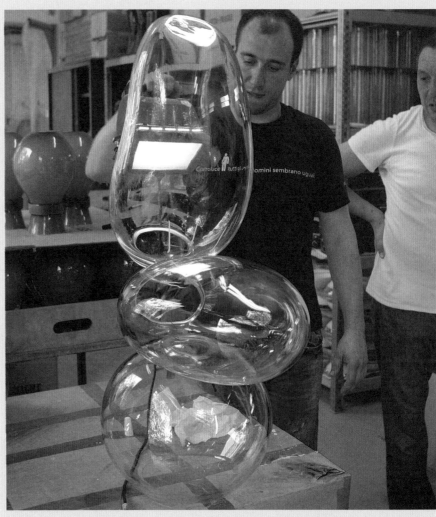

Re-thinking the Obvious
The Hallion – LWD

The use of glass as mirror is well established in interior design and, conventionally, it is used to give an accurate reflection of the room that contains it. While straight reflection may be no more than a mundane attempt to increase the perceived size of the room, interestingly edited images may be created – incidentally by an observer's particular viewpoint, or deliberately, by angling a mirror off the face of a wall.

The bespoke mirror on the wall of the dining room develops the idea of the fragmented image. It breaks the total mirrored area into a mosaic of much smaller mirrors that make an almost abstract composition. An outer plane of mirrors are supported on short stalks with connecting joints that allow them to be angled and, if considered necessary, adjusted to change the composition of the reflection. The wall behind the adjustable grid is also mirrored to increase the apparent depth and complexity of the image.

Above
Glass mirrors are better than plastic mirrors, which, though cheaper and much lighter, warp easily and distort the image. This faceted example becomes a powerful object regardless of the nature of its reflected image.

Left
The near-abstract fragmentation makes the image more intriguing than a conventional flat reflection.

Below
Individual mirrors are rotated on a universal joint, and the back of each is also mirrored, as is the wall behind, to make multilayered images.

Stone

The range of stone types offers a complex palette of colours, patterns and textures. It can be used in its roughly cut 'raw' state or, as is more frequently the case with furniture, in thin slabs polished on one face to accentuate its natural colours and patterns. It is most commonly used as table and counter tops but it is important to check its absorbency when, as in a bar, liquids and organic materials may be spilt on it and result in discoloured and unhygienic surfaces. Marble, with a swirling linear pattern, and granite, with a speckled pattern, are most frequently used. Both offer a wide colour range.

Small stones are used as 'aggregate', along with sand and cement, in the making of concrete. Although usually hidden within the mass of concrete, the aggregate may be exposed for heightened texture by washing or grinding away the smooth, very thin, outer surface of sand and cement. To achieve this effect, aggregate should be specially selected for its colour and shape. A similar process is used to make 'terrazzo', in which marble chips, selected for colour and size, are used as aggregate but exposed by grinding and polishing so that the chips are cut through and their exposed sections provide the colour and pattern. All such materials must be sealed to eliminate dust. Finished slabs may be used as table and counter tops. Outdoor furniture can be produced in moulds.

Increasingly, reconstituted stone, made of ground stone dust and a binding agent, is used because it is cheap and uses waste material from more conventional stone-cutting techniques. When formed in a mould, it is useful as a replacement for carved stone and in moulded furniture, where comfort and mobility are not primary concerns. Additives can reduce weight.

Fired clays produce a material normally described as ceramic and most frequently used in tile form. Tiles come in standard sizes and this can be a crucial factor in determining the dimensions of, for example, a tabletop or counter front. The very visible joints make any divergence from standard sizes very obvious. They have the advantage of having fixed sizes and being thinner and lighter than stone. Glazed finishes offer enormous variety of colour and pattern. Moulds offer surface textures. Variations in sizes and finishes may be made to order and, as always, the economics of this depend on the number required.

Textiles

In furniture design textiles are primarily used for upholstery but ingenious responses to particular briefs may find that some less traditional types offer interesting opportunities. New woven textiles in particular have great strength and, when stretched taut, form smooth, resilient surfaces.

Textiles derived from natural sources may broadly be subdivided into those woven from animal products, such as wool and silk, and those from plant sources, such as cotton, flax, jute, hemp and sisal. Again, environmental concerns have introduced additional selection criteria. Some, like cotton, which is produced on a massive scale in hot countries, require large quantities of water both for irrigation when growing and in the manufacturing processes. In contrast, flax grows naturally in wet climates and its production is less industrialized and less polluting, if only because it sells in much smaller quantities. Wool is virtuous because it is essentially a by-product of the meat industry.

Synthetic petroleum-based textiles are also considered acceptable since, as by-products of the oil industry, they utilize what would otherwise be a polluting waste product. Synthetics can be manufactured with harder-wearing properties, better stain-resistance and a degree of elasticity.

Below
An interpretation of a traditional wing-backed chair: the black mesh stretched over the steel frame forms cushioned headrests and complex patterns when superimposed.

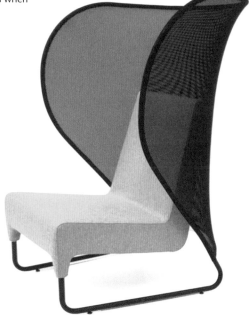

Left
A reinforced plastic/paper made of high-density polyethylene fibre, used in the building industry, is stretched over a wire frame – like a Japanese lantern – and inflated. It resonates like a drum.

Metal meshes, which use textile weaving techniques, have a durability that makes them appropriate for furniture applications. Although stronger than cloth, fine meshes can be as pliable. Others are progressively more rigid as the diameter of 'threads' or the width of flat strips increases.

Textiles can now incorporate digital technology and offer options for fabrics that contain light and heat sources and can react to the presence of users.

Geosynthetics, composites typically made from polypropylene or polyester and used in environmental engineering, offer robust options suitable for use in locations alien to conventional textiles.

Upholstery

While there is, inevitably, some substitution of modern materials for old – foam for horsehair or coir as stuffing, and staples and staple guns for dome-headed pins and hammers – traditional upholstery techniques remain as relevant for the production of good-quality new pieces as they do for restoration. Apart from the additional comfort, an advantage of upholstery is that concealed framing does not require a high standard of finish.

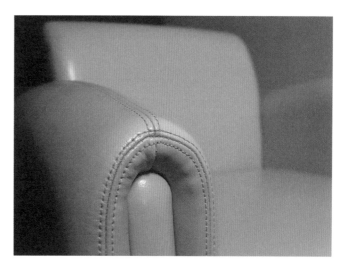

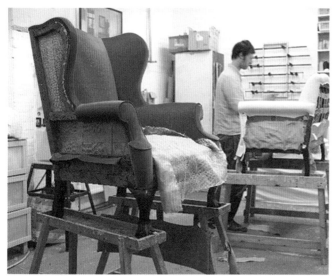

Left
In traditional upholstery a wooden frame establishes the form. Padding is added in thicknesses appropriate to the parts and posture of the body in contact with it. Loose padding materials are held in place by horizontal and vertical webbing strips and strengthened in the seat by springs tied in position. The finishing textile is laid over a loosely woven intermediary fabric, usually hessian, and held in position by small round-headed nails. It is gathered evenly at corners and curves and exposed edges are doubled inwards.

Above
Leather covering is usually stitched by hand or machine. It is difficult to work. As in textile upholstery, the pattern caused by fixing should be considered at the design stage. Since dimensions of pieces of leather are inevitably smaller than rolls of fabric, the seams are likely to be more frequent.

Above
Wrapping a structural frame, for reasons of comfort and aesthetics, opens extraordinary possibilities.

Below
Textiles, particularly those with stretch capacity, adapt well to unfamiliar forms and applications, in this case also covering the inverted conical legs.

Top
New materials emerge with ever greater speed. Designers' impulse is to find ways to use them and, from that, new forms also emerge. In this chair the irregular mesh of the structural frame is sandwiched between two layers of the fabric.

Above
The doubling over of fabric for the back and seat is treated casually, with no attempt to achieve the rigid precision of traditional upholstery. The transverse connection between the front leg and its diagonally opposite number provides cross-bracing without interfering with the spindly verticals.

Applied finishes

The appearance of materials may be changed for aesthetic reasons or to give protection against corrosion and degradation. Most of the finishes commonly used in furniture making provide both. For internal use, paint is primarily a colouring agent and can be applied to timber, metal and plastic surfaces. It is normal to paint all softwood pieces for preservation and because their surface quality tends to be of variable quality. Gloss finish, which is easier to clean than matt or semi-gloss, is most frequently used for furniture; application using a spray gun ensures a more even finish than hand-painting. Cellulose-based paints, particularly if applied to an MDF base, give a particularly smooth and dense finish. Other paints give a range of textures and surface reflectivity.

Stains, both water-based and oil-based, change the hue of timber and enhance rather than conceal its natural grain. They preserve the natural matt surface. Varnishes are oil-based and also enhance colour and grain with a more resilient surface and a gloss or semi-gloss finish.

Timber surfaces can be oiled or waxed, which protects against moisture and accentuates grain patterns. This is a traditional method, used primarily on hardwood components, and must be renewed at regular intervals.

Mild steel needs to be protected against moisture, even in interiors. It can be sealed with oil or a clear varnish. Both will darken its natural light-grey colour.

The same fabric on the same shell can be coloured to suit its context.

Fixings

Specialist glues, particular to each of the materials commonly used in furniture making, provide an invisible fixing that is usually stronger than the mechanical options of nails, panel pins, screws, nuts, bolts and washers. As their properties become refined and their setting times are reduced, their use becomes more widespread. The mechanical options may, however, be favoured for aesthetic reasons. Since all components in the range of standard fixings will normally cope with all eventualities, the criteria for selection are primarily aesthetic. Each device and technique makes a distinctive contribution to defining detail.

Nails, panel pins and screws are suitable only for use with timber or timber-based products. The first two can damage the surface into which they are driven and are therefore mostly used in concealed locations. When oval nail and panel pinheads can be punched below the surface of the timber the recess may be filled, sanded and painted to eliminate evidence of its existence.

Screws are distinguished from nails by the raised, helical 'thread' that runs along the greater part of their length. The circular movement generated by a screwdriver causes the ridges of the thread to cut into the core of timber and the integration of thread and wood means that a screw makes a significantly stronger connection than a nail.

Nuts and bolts may be used to secure timber, metal and glass components. Bolts, like screws, are threaded but have a blunt rather than a pointed end and pass through aligned pre-drilled holes in the elements they connect. They are secured by a threaded nut on the reverse side. Pre-drilled holes normally have a bigger diameter than the bolts to allow some tolerance during fixing. Washers fit neatly over the bolts to cover the gap and to spread the load.

Nails

It is difficult to ensure precision in the use of nails because hammering is a less easily controlled activity than screwing and is therefore more likely to damage the wood and less suited to the delicate process of furniture-making. Small-headed panel pins, which may be fixed with gentle tapping were widely used to fix thin sheets in position while glues dried, but faster-setting, stronger modern glues are increasingly making them redundant. Larger nails are more likely to be used where they will not be visible – as in the assembly of framing – but when visible it is important to specify their precise location and spacing. For example, with the rectangular-headed nail, the orientation of the rectangular head should be made clear. Even if a nominally random pattern is required, this must be specified and rules set out, otherwise the joiner will naturally fall into a regular rhythm.

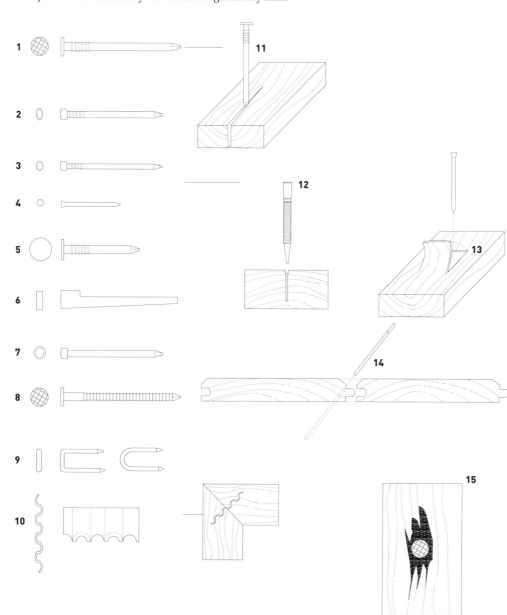

1   Flat-head wire nail – for general joinery work, probably the most familiar type but unlikely to be used in furniture-making, unless the round head is used decoratively.
2   Oval brad or bullet head – used in general joinery. If the long axis of the oval runs parallel to the grain it will be less likely to split the wood.
3   Lost head nail – used in general carpentry. The head can be driven below the wood surface.
4   Panel pin – used with glue.
5   Clout nail – normally used externally in roofing and fencing but the large galvanized head can be used decoratively.
6   Flooring or cut nail – the rectangular head can be used decoratively.
7   Masonry nail – hardened steel for fixing timber to brick and concrete blocks. It may be used when fixing furniture to, or hanging it off, a wall.
8   Annular ring shank – used for fixing panels such as plywood. The rings make them very difficult to remove.
9   Wire staple – mostly used in upholstery.
10 Wood cleat – for butt or mitre joints when a quick or lightweight joint is required.
11 Wire nails have a tendency to split wood – blunting the tip can help prevent this.
12 Panel pins and lost head nails can be driven below the timber surface with a nail punch. The hole can then be filled and sanded smooth.
13 A nail head can also be concealed by chiselling back a thin sliver of wood, driving the nail into and below the surface in the recess and gluing back the sliver, sanding it if necessary, flush with the surface of the wood.
14 Flooring or cut nails are driven at an angle into the 'tongue' of a board and will then be covered by the 'groove' of the next board. This is called 'secret fixing'.
15 Steel nails should not be used with timbers, such as oak, that have a high tannin content. Tannic acid reacts with steel to form a brown stain. Stainless-steel or brass nails should be used.

Screws

Electric drills and screwdrivers now make the process of inserting screws as fast as nailing. Standard practice is to pre-drill holes for screws, with a 'bit', or cutting point, with a diameter slightly smaller than that of the screw. Screws are easier to remove than nails, by reversing the direction of the screwdriver, but a visible hole will be left.

Screws are normally steel with a protective coating to prevent rust; zinc is the most common finish although even this is unsuitable for external use or in areas of high humidity, which require a hot galvanized finish. Stainless steel will resist corrosion but lacks tensile strength; a black oxide finish provides some protection for stronger screws. Brass screws are frequently used in furniture for aesthetic reasons but are also useful when used with woods, such as oak, which have a high tannin content that will corrode steel. Brass is soft, however, and care must be taken that the screwdriver does not deform the head. It is also a sound precaution to make the diameter of the pre-drilled hole slightly larger than for a steel screw.

There are many varieties of screw heads. Some are necessarily selected for practical reasons but aesthetic considerations are as important. The metal used in manufacture and finish and the screw size should be specified. Size is defined by length and a number, which relates to the diameter of the threaded shaft. Each length is available in a range of numbers. Larger screw sizes are normally used with larger timber sections. Drill bit diameters are numbered to match screw sizes.

Types of screw head

1. Wood screw: a) thread. b) shank (the unthreaded shanke allows one piece of wood to be drawn tight against another without catching the thread. c) head.
2. Drywall screw (used primarily for fixing gypsum plasterboard to timber or metal stud framework in partition walls but offer a black finish for other applications): a) thread. b) head.
3. Sheet metal screw (used for fixing thin metal sheet and threads are more closely spaced): a) thread. b) head.
4. Hex.

Types of screwdriver

5. Slotted.
6. Posidrive.
7. Phillips.
8. Allen key.
9. Torx.
10. Security T.

Screw head profiles

11. Countersunk (flat).
12. Double countersunk.
13. Double countersunk (oval raised).
14. Bugle head.
15. Domed round head.
16. Button head.
17. Pan head.
18. Hex head.

Screw fixing techniques

Given the modest scale of furniture and users' intimate interaction with it, decisions about types of screw and their application are crucial in defining aesthetics. In most applications where screw heads remain visible it is desirable for reasons of both appearance and practicality for them to finish flush with the face of the wood. Driving screws into the wood until they are flush, which is normal practice in carcassing work, will result in damage to the wood around the head. To avoid this an inverted conical recess can be formed by a countersinking drill bit; this accommodates the inverted conical profile of the screw head and allows the top of the head to sit flush with the surface of the wood. Some screws, with a flat interface with the wood and a dome-shaped head, can be used with a small, normally metal, washer between the screw and the wood surface to mask peripheral damage to the wood. Raised circular metal rings or 'cups' may be used as cushions and spacers to keep screw heads above the face of wood, and to conceal damage caused during the tightening process.

Heads may also be entirely concealed within pre-drilled recesses, with a diameter large enough to accommodate them and the appropriate screwdriver point. When the screw is tightened, the recess is closed with a wooden plug cut and sanded to finish flush with the surface of the component it is securing. Plugs are generally made with a specialist bit that cuts them from the same wood as that into which they will be inserted with their tone and grain providing a near invisible seal. Ready-made plugs are available in a range of timbers, but they are unlikely to provide an exact match. It may therefore be preferable to use a distinctly different wood and to make a virtue of the discrepancy by creating a pattern of highly visible plugs. Ready-made plugs are normally slightly tapered with the narrower end inserted first and the plug hammered tight before the projecting portion is planed off flush with the timber face.

Visible screws

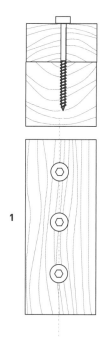

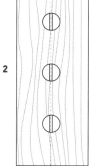
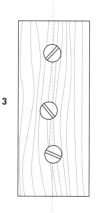
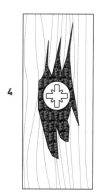

1 The screw head sits on the surface of the wood. If it is not big enough to cover local damage, caused by drill, screwdriver or over-tightening of the screw, then a washer should be inserted between it and the wood.
2 A countersunk screw head will finish flush with the surface of the wood and the countersinking bit should eliminate peripheral damage.
3 When heads are visible, even spacing and alignment should be specified.
4 Over-tightening of the screw can cause surface damage to the wood. Staining may be caused by rust or chemical reaction between metal and wood.

Countersinking the head

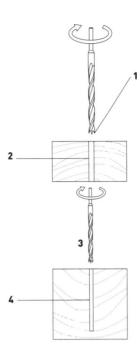

1 In the piece of timber against which the screw head will be tightened, the bit size should match that of the screw to allow the screw to pass easily through the first piece before engaging fully with the second. A wood twist bit has a fluted end cutter that will scribe the wood before the main body of the bit begins to enter the wood, preventing splitting and ensuring a cleaner hole.
2 The hole should offer no resistance either to the threaded or smooth section of the screw.
3 A bit sized smaller than the screw should be used in the timber to receive the screw thread.
4 The smaller hole eases the screw's passage into the wood but allows the raised threads to interlock securely with it.

Concealing the head

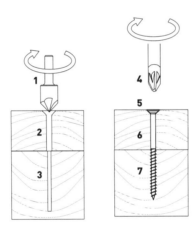

1 A countersinking bit cuts an inverted conical recess to receive the screw head.
2 Hole to match the diameter of the screw to receive smooth shaft.
3 Smaller diameter hole to receive threaded shaft.
4 Screwdriver point to suit screw head.
5 Countersinking screw head.
6 Smooth screw shaft.
7 Threaded screw shaft.

Preparing the wood

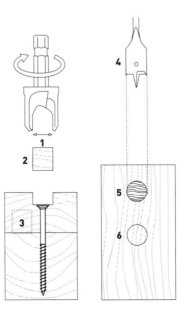

1 A drill bit to cut and remove 'plug'.
2 Wooden plug.
3 Plugs may be cut from places that will not be visible in the finished piece. Using the same piece of wood ensures, as far as is possible in an organic material, a match of tone and texture.
4 A drill bit that matches the diameter of the plug.
5 A recess for the screw and plug.
6 The plug should provide a near-invisible cover.

Bolts and machine screws

While they may be used to connect timber elements bolts and machine screws are most commonly used to connect metal with metal. Bolts may also be used to connect plastics or glass, with a resilient washer to prevent cracking when the nut is tightened. There is some ambiguity about exact definitions of each but it is perhaps acceptable to say that bolts are passed through pre-drilled holes in two elements and their threaded end section receives a nut that is tightened to lock the elements together. A machine screw also has a threaded end section but this is inserted into a 'tapped' hole, pre-drilled with a compatible thread. Both come with a variety of heads and selection is likely to be an aesthetic one since both are stout enough to deal with furniture's structural demands. Countersinking in metals, although obviously a more difficult procedure than in wood, is possible if carried out in a specialist metal workshop.

Types of bolt and machine screw

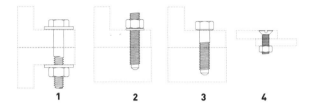

1   Bolt with nut and washers.
2   Stud machine screw.
3   Cap machine screw.
4   Countersunk bolt and nut.

Types of machine screw head

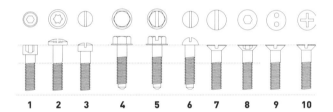

1   Allen key socket.
2   Cheese heap torx.
3   Slotted fillster.
4   Hex.
5   Hex-head slotted.
6   Dome-head slotted.
7   Countersunk slotted.
8   Countersunk Allen key.
9   Countersunk pig-nosed.
10 Countersunk Phillips.

Set screws

A set screw is used to lock elements together with a minimum visual presence. It is tightened within a tapped hole and designed to finish flush with surfaces. Although designed to be visually unobtrusive there are options for the visible area of the head.

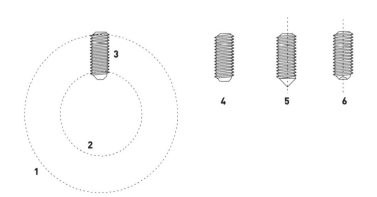

Set screw in threaded hole in outer tube, pressing against the inner element when fully tightened.
1   Outer element.
2   Inner element.
3   Set screw.
4   Flat point.
5   Cone point.
6   Cup point.

Fittings

Visible fittings, like handles and hinges, are the final component that defines the character and quality of a furniture piece. Important as they are, there are very few occasions when it makes practical or economic sense to design and make something so intricate and, often, complex given the range of commercially manufactured options. This is another instance in which the designer's knowledge of generic types available helps with the initial narrowing, based on practical priorities, of the field for a final selection, based on aesthetic criteria. Often when searching for a particular fitting one will discover an alternative that will suggest positive amendments to the whole piece.

There are other fittings that are designed to remain, for the most part, unseen, like drawer runners and locks and, when they do appear in the course of a piece's operation, they are excused the obligation to look anything more than efficient.

The examples illustrated offer an abbreviated glimpse of some of the generic categories of products available. Inevitably the companies involved in their production maintain websites showing their complete range. Some also provide downloads of each item so that these can be pasted into detail drawings, which saves drawing time and ensures accuracy in the related detail.

Hinges

Decisions about an appropriate hinge type initially depend on how a door is to open and shut and the degree to which it is acceptable to see the hinge. Unless a door is very heavy or the hinges very delicate it is normally enough to have two hinges, top and bottom, for a door. The number of screws can vary and is determined by the configuration of the selected hinge. Screws are normally the same material and colour as the hinge, usually brass, stainless steel or nickel and chrome plated steel. Generic examples are shown here.

1   Piano hinge. This usually runs the full length of a vertical or horizontal pivoting edge. It is available in various lengths and thicknesses, with or without screw holes. The continuous 'knuckle' is often used for aesthetic reasons.

2   Butt hinge.

3   Cranked hinge. Used where the door leaf sits in front of rather than inside the frame.

4   Table or counter-flap hinge. A hinge that sits flush with the horizontal surface of counter or tabletop allowing a panel to be pivoted through 180 degrees for access.

5   Concealed hinge – also called the Cup or Euro. Most commonly used in kitchen cabinets and may be sprung or 'soft closing', which is controlled gradual closure, They are made in two parts, a mounting plate that fixes onto the cabinet frame and a hinge and 'cup' that fits into a pre-drilled hole in the door. They have the great advantage of being adjustable, both in distance off the face of the cabinet and in the vertical, allowing finely tuned adjustments to allow even flush spacing of door leaves. Different models allow the door to be full overlay (a), half overlay (b) or inset (c).

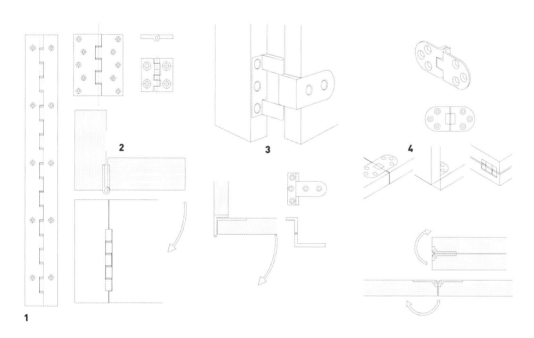

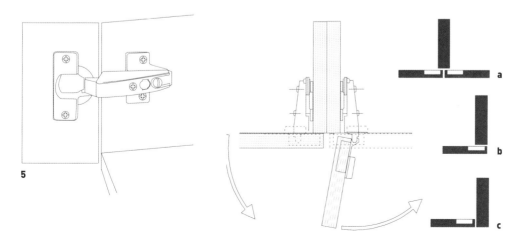

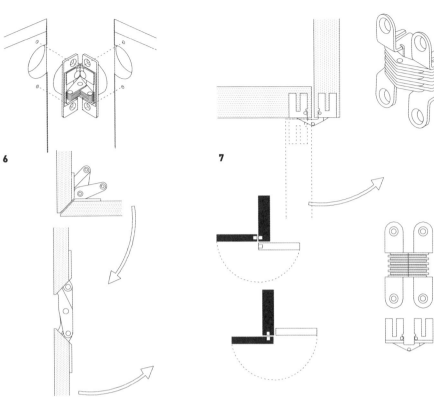

6   Mitred concealed hinge. creates an almost invisible junction between door and cabinet.

7   Concealed or Soss hinge. Allows 180-degree opening and is available in a range of sizes that will support heavier doors than the Euro will.

8   Pivot hinge. Concealed in the top and bottom edges of the door. The pivot action requires the door to be set forward of the side panel of the cabinet or have a radiused inside edge to allow it to open and shut.

9   Drill-in hinge. A pivot hinge fitted to the edge of the door and cabinet.

10   Door flap stay. Available in a number of configurations, from sprung to pneumatic, holds open a hinged panel and prevents it opening beyond a fixed point. It may be used horizontally or vertically and for top and bottom hanging.

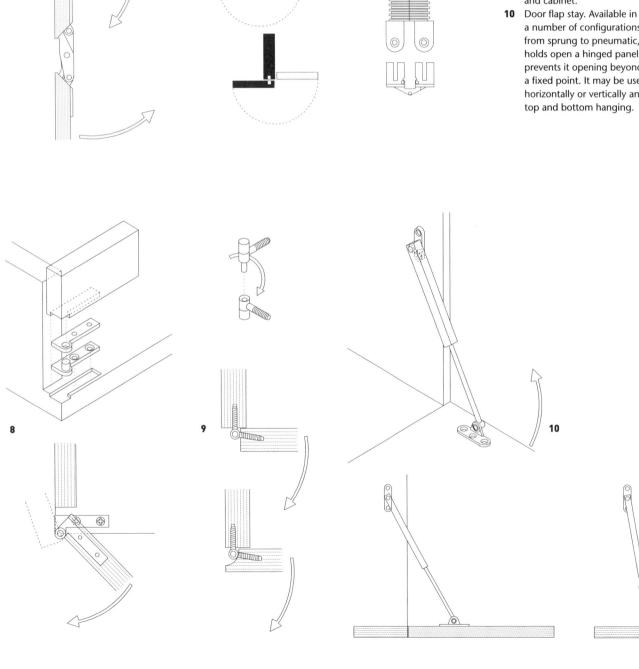

Drawer runners

The simple wooden runners that could be made by any capable joiner have been superseded by the more complex, factory-produced examples that incorporate wheels in tracks for smoother running, stops and, increasingly, soft, or pneumatically controlled, closing. While exposure of the mechanism is usually acceptable a more refined hidden track makes possible unsullied drawer sides.

1 Traditional wooden runner. Construction needs to use solid wood, to allow for the necessary rigidity and routing, and is therefore heavy but very robust. A simpler version has runners beneath the drawer sides.

2 Roller action. Drawer construction, usually from veneered chipboard, is lightweight with aluminium runners and tracks. The wheels remain static, fixed to the side of the cabinet and the runner, fixed to the side of the drawer rolls over them. The closed relationship is indicated as A and the open as B.

3 Concealed runners. When open, track is concealed by the drawer sides.

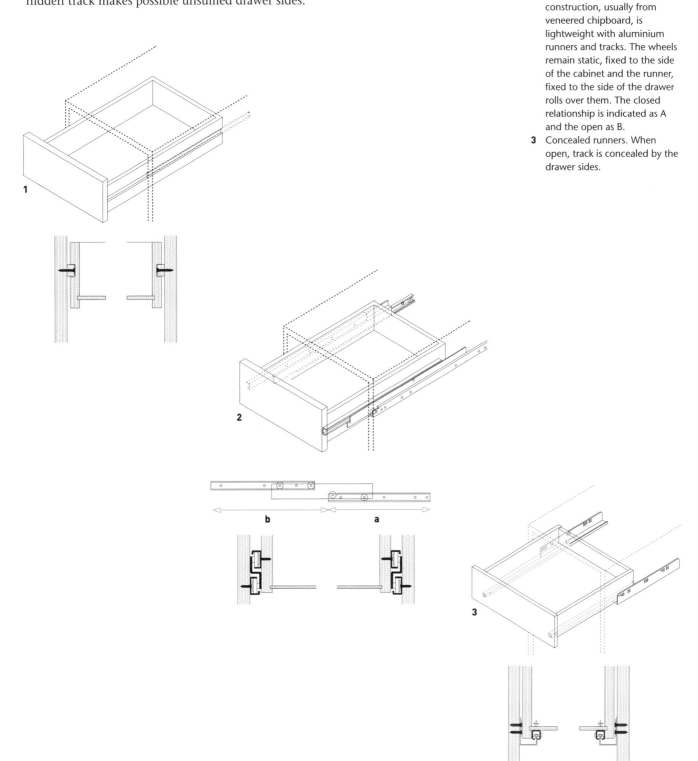

PART 4 WORKING ON A PROJECT

The forms and components of furniture are tried and tested and need no fundamental revision but it is a designer's responsibility to refresh the familiar and to enrich the commonplace. While this may prompt a dramatic gesture, it will never justify a gratuitous one. Transformation is likely to be evolutionary, involving minor variations.

New directions will not necessarily be found in furniture precedents but are as likely to be inspired by divergent thinking that illuminates the problem in hand. Initial strategic decisions should be made for aesthetic reasons and subsequent decisions about the practicalities of construction should conform to, and enhance, those first perceptions. A designer's instinct is always to preserve intact that first vision and thinking can thus become hermetic and it is not unreasonable to suggest that, if there are no significant changes to the first proposition, the final outcome is likely to be flawed because the problems – and potential – inherent and inevitable in those raw first thoughts have not been identified and dealt with. Designers should question the validity of their decision-making if they find they are habitually coming to the same conclusion.

The creative process is conducted within a designer's imagination and, if it goes unchallenged, will drift into familiar reiterative territory. On the other hand, practical hurdles, if confronted positively, will nudge the imagination towards the unfamiliar. The conceptual idea comes intuitively and quickly, and by far the greater proportion of designing time will, or should, be devoted to resolving practicalities. The priority should continue to be aesthetic – this is not to say that function and sound construction can be sacrificed, but rather to recognize that there is more than one way to achieve a satisfactory resolution of practical issues.

Visual detailing, which ultimately defines the character of any piece of furniture, does not need to be complex to be good. Some construction details that are crucial to the expression of the concept may not be visible at all. Whether visually important or not, all detailing requires the same degree of willingness on the part of the designer to struggle with the conundrums it presents.

Many of the essential techniques of designing are common, to a greater or lesser degree, to all design disciplines and this is particularly true of interior design and furniture design. The materials and detailing methods that make interior spaces are different, with a very few exceptions, from those that make furniture and very few designers can have comprehensive knowledge of specialist making techniques. However, an understanding of the capacities of the most commonly used materials provides a solid foundation upon which to build.

Inexperienced designers tend to be wary of detailing. They find it easier to be confident about a conceptual idea, which is no more than a matter of opinion, than they are about detailing, which is obliged to satisfy verifiable practicalities. It can be disturbing to realize that the particular complexity of each site-specific piece is likely to introduce factors that preclude the application of standard solutions.

Even designers who work to keep abreast of technical developments cannot always have the perceptions that come from practical experience of their application, and they will know that they cannot be aware of every recent advance in every field. Ultimately the essential skill they need is to be able to see the possibilities that new materials and techniques offer. They need to have the visual and verbal expertise to ask questions effectively of those, be they cabinetmakers, metalworkers, upholsterers or plastic polymer scientists, who have the requisite specialist knowledge.

Tyro designers experience uncertainty, but once they have proposed, detailed and have had a number of projects of varying degrees of difficulty completed and once they have taken part in the dialogues, with clients, makers and suppliers, that lead to successful conclusions, they will find the confidence that will allow them to propose and pursue successfully ever more ambitious ideas.

Design development

A successful interior and the furniture that will complete it emerges from an understanding of the needs of the client and the realities of an existing building.

Understanding the brief

Clients know what they want but often this is expressed in the broadest of terms and based on preconceptions that deserve to be gently challenged. Some will give the designer room to speculate and some will be uncomfortable with the unfamiliar. Briefs are often very brief. To the client, utterly involved with the project, the requirements may seem too obvious to need stating in detail but for the designer, it is crucial to get a comprehensive understanding of client needs and expectations, and an experienced designer will instantly have a stream of questions to clarify operational details that are ambiguous or that would appear to have been overlooked.

An initial dialogue between designer and client can define content precisely, allow each an insight into the other's priorities and set a precedent for collaborative discussion that should continue throughout the project. Whatever the project, the client will have essential information about functional requirements, probably opinions about the aesthetic direction and strong views about the budget. If the first brief is perfunctory, a more detailed subsequent agreement on content and responsibility, which evolves in discussions, should be recorded and agreed in writing by both parties.

Perceptions will, and should, change during project development and the client needs to be informed and consulted about deviations from original intentions. The process of explanation and persuasion will help test the validity of shifts in thinking. Frequent meetings about progress concentrate the designer's mind and encourage creative adrenalin.

Clients should be sound on practical matters, and therefore able to see the value of suggested improvements. Their own insights into how their interiors should function are valuable but usually fall within predictable areas with which designers are familiar or about which they can make further productive speculation. A client will have crucial insights about how their employees work: not just what tasks are performed but the sequence in which they are carried out. It is valuable to think about the needs of the 'extended' client, those who will use furniture as employees or as customers. It is valuable to canvass them directly.

Understanding the site
Making a measured survey

Interior designers work within existing physical structures that are filled with possibilities or limitations. Surveying is about dimensions but also about understanding materials and services, natural lighting and acoustics. An accurate measured survey is essential, both for organizing the most efficient furniture layouts and establishing the context for built-in pieces. Accuracy is particularly important when designing fitted pieces to be manufactured off site. Small discrepancies can translate into big problems on site.

Drawings of the original building may exist but their accuracy should always be questioned. Buildings are never constructed exactly as drawn by their original designer. Dimensions should never be taken from existing drawings; they may not be accurate in the first instance and paper stretches and contracts.

Hand-held laser-measuring devices are increasingly replacing tapes as surveying tools, allowing one person to take dimensions quickly and extremely accurately. A tilt sensor will measure a true horizontal distance over an obstruction or into inaccessible spaces. Some models transmit dimensions to laptops where speculative plans and elevations will be resized automatically.

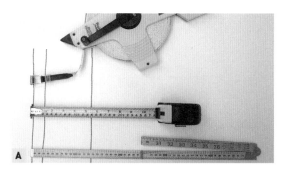

A Traditional tape measures. A self-retracting metal tape measure serves for horizontal and vertical dimensions up to 5m/16ft, and a fibreglass surveyor's tape for long 'running' dimensions.

B A metal tape laid across the window recess represents the line of the face of the wall – for measuring the depth of the recess.

C A telescopic measuring rod gives readings within restricted spaces.

D Dimensions are shown in an analogue display.

Note-taking

An A4 sheet will be enough to record the data from most rooms. Significant areas and details can be drawn at a larger scale and referenced to the main drawing. All sheets should be numbered because they will be referred to throughout the design process.

A compact digital camera or smart phone will provide images to clarify discrepancies in the drawing.

An empty building may well have had its electricity disconnected. An LED head torch leaves hands free for drawing. Abandoned buildings can be dirty and dangerous and should only be entered after taking advice and wearing appropriate clothing – and never alone.

STEP BY STEP SURVEYING A BUILDING

From photographs made on a first site visit it is possible to extrapolate a proportioned plan drawing to which measured data may be added. It is easier to make the base drawing at a well-lit desk than on a clipboard in a dimly lit building in uncomfortable conditions.

Measurements, which record the distance of each significant point from the fixed datum, should be made in a clockwise direction and recorded as 'running' dimensions, to avoid the aggregation of error that occurs with multiple small, single measurements.

'Running' dimensions should be written in metres; an accuracy of +/- 5mm/¼in is acceptable. More detailed dimensions taken from point to point, such as the depth of a doorframe, are recorded in millimetres between a 'crossed line' indicating the points measured.

Heights are also recorded in millimetres, and written in a circle to differentiate them from plan measurements. A sequence of heights, such as ceiling, window head and windowsill, is recorded within the same circle but divided by horizontal lines with the highest at the top.

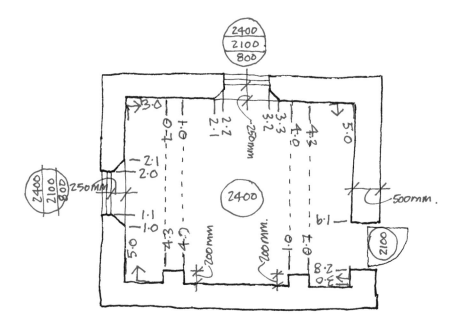

1 Plan dimensions are usually taken at a height of 1200mm/47¼in above the floor. This will cut through most windows, which are obviously crucially relevant. Details or areas of specific interest are drawn at a larger scale with dimensions taken point to point.

2 Separate larger-scale drawings for crucial areas should be cross-referenced on the overall plan.

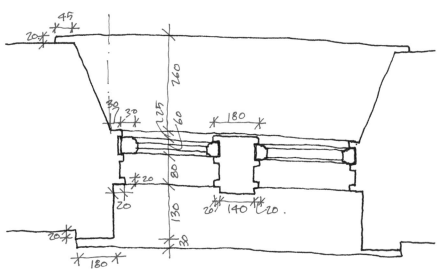

Section: Plan window A

TIP DRAWING UP THE SURVEY

Graphic conventions should be adhered to. Minor variations may be introduced, according to taste, but divergence from the recognized norms is dangerous. Dotted and dashed lines should be used to communicate details above 1200mm/47¼in. Dashed lines should be used to indicate low-level, hidden elements. The location of elements such as power sockets and light switches should be represented by recognized symbols.

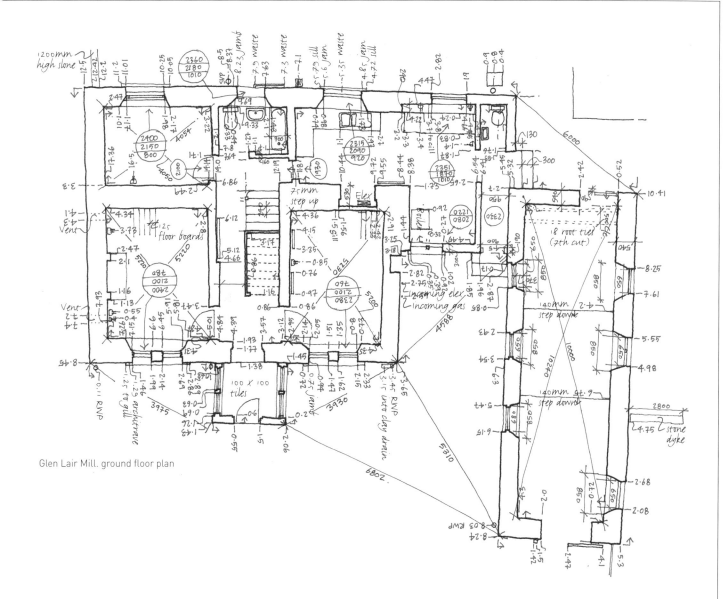

Glen Lair Mill. ground floor plan

3 Assume that corners will not be right angles. Diagonal dimensions taken from opposing corners can be used to confirm the angle of the intersection of the two walls it connects. Diagonal dimensions provide the information necessary to establish angles. Survey notes should be checked before leaving the site. It is usually possible to extrapolate internal elevations from the plan and heights. More complicated elevations or sections should be measured. If external elevations are needed, it is more efficient to measure down from the eaves (the point at which the roof meets the wall) as this will normally be level, while the ground will not.

TIP MEASURING WALL THICKNESSES

In traditional construction the width of the frame will equal that of the wall and the architrave moulding will cover the junction of the two. Therefore measuring the distance between the inside edges of architraves will give the wall thickness. Similar extrapolations can be made for non-traditional detailing.

Visualizing the proposal

A designer's first instinct when beginning a project is to start to draw, whether by computer or by hand. When you are presented with a new brief, a first idea is liable to insinuate itself spontaneously into the imagination. It is likely to be a simple transference of ideas used in previous projects but will serve as a starting point for objective deliberation. If first thoughts are committed too quickly to paper or screen, they can lock the imagination into a direction with inherent problems which it will be difficult to identify and more difficult to discard. It is wiser to postpone visualization, to think in broader, more abstract terms, to establish criteria that will prompt sharper questions and establish a context in which answers may be better assessed.

If progress stalls, it can be productive to revert to thinking without drawing until a new direction is established. Hand-drawing in particular tends to drift into repetition, with the mind becoming more engaged with refining the drawing than developing its content. Quality of sketching is of no importance. Drawings that encapsulate significant ideas are normally crude because they are made spontaneously.

If freehand drawings normally represent the first steps in the design process, move quickly to making scaled drawings, to establish and assess exact proportions. The first scaled drawings are often disappointing. They expose weaknesses in proportions that were fudged in optimistic sketches. Computers convert two-dimensional drawings immediately to three dimensions, render materials and colours accurately, and allow images to be rotated for scrutiny in virtual space.

Ultimately interiors and the pieces of furniture within them are the evidence by which the design process will be assessed. Drawings are of no lasting consequence. Drawing by hand has advocates who believe in a creative symbiosis between hand and brain. Younger designers better understand and exploit digital drawing. Individuals need to find the way of working that best suits their way of thinking.

An experienced designer will begin, from the very first idea, to think about detailing options and their visual impact. Crucial to the process will be decisions about materials, based on considerations of practical performance and aesthetic compatibility. Often the final proposal will adhere closely to first expectations but alternatives should emerge consistently throughout the design process, as the nature of the proposal becomes clearer.

Developments should, where possible, be discussed with the client at regular intervals, to ensure that a new direction is approved. The representation of ideas, whether in drawn or model form, will become progressively more refined and detailed. The final presentation will explain what the client can expect and, if approved, it is the designer's job to produce a set of 'production drawings'. The number of these will vary from project to project but their function remains constant, to provide the maker with a comprehensive description in drawings and words of the full extent and quality of the work commissioned and to form the basis of the contractual agreement between client and maker.

Cross-fertilization
Glyndebourne Restaurant – Nigel Coates Studio

Ideas for different elements within a project can cross-fertilize. The concept for the waiter stations in the restaurant at Glyndebourne began as a proposal to stack circular tables around columns. The lowest would accommodate the practical elements of the station and the upper levels would hold decorative artefacts. The straight legs of the first sketch evolved in response to those of a chair designed for the same restaurant (see p.176) and the relative heights of the shelves related to that of the objects which each held.

Above
The first idea, to stack tables around columns.

Right
The legs evolve in response to those of the chair.

Left
The bent leg becomes the defining and linking element of both waiter stations and chairs.

Above
The upper shelves support a variety of objects that become a decorative cladding to the original column.

Prototypes and mock-ups

Every furniture piece has a function, however nominal. If it does not, it is reduced to the status of abstract sculpture. Its function will give its designer and those who view or use it common ground for communication and because it has to be functional, it must take as its starting point basic anthropometric and ergonomic data. These are necessarily generalizations since humans vary in size and physical capabilities, and a designer may stretch and compress dimensions for effect. Testing simple prototypes may assess the feasibility of juggling, however modestly, with prescribed dimensions. It is possible to assess the viability of variations by understanding the movement and rhythms of those who will use the piece. Variation to suit the physical particularities of a single prescribed user is easily verified. With multiple users, standard dimensional data may be less easily discarded.

Prototypes need not be constructed from the same materials as the proposed finished piece, nor is it always necessary to represent them in their entirety. If the intention is to assess proportion, which usually happens early in the process, the prototype need have no more strength than is required to hold its shape. Cheap composite boards, even corrugated cardboard, will serve. When ergonomics and anthropometrics are being tested, however, the prototype must be capable of supporting the weight of users and objects that will be placed on it. Materials and joints must be strong enough not only to support anticipated loads but, where appropriate, vigorous movements. Prototypes for both these tests may be made cursorily, in the studio or general workshop, but when the aesthetics of materials and details are to be assessed, then the same quality of making is necessary and will require specialist input. The whole object need not necessarily be made: junctions and fixings may be enough.

Rough models may be enough to communicate aspects of early thinking to a client but, for a final presentation, they must be precise enough to confirm that the process has been properly concluded. As with a model of an interior space, it is difficult to represent the texture and pattern of materials accurately to scale and so a monochromatic model may best represent the three-dimensional form. A model can

A & B An adjustable trolley facilitated investigation of optimum heights for museum cabinets.

C & D Trials find a height that works for ambulant visitors and wheelchair users.

Above
Materials and joints must replicate those of the intended finished piece if the prototype is to produce accurate information about practical performance.

Far left
A full-size prototype allows comprehensive assessment.

Left
When the prototype can support loads, anthropometric and ergonomic efficiency can be assessed.

be sprayed any hue but white will maximize the defining qualities of light and shade. Where the relationships between different components become crucial in understanding proportions and materiality, then colours can be used to identify elements. These should be close enough to the materials they represent to avoid confusion but even perfectly matched hues and tones will behave differently at different scales.

Appropriate scales will vary throughout the process. The first exploratory versions may be very small – just large enough to answer simple first questions about general configuration. They can also be full size, to test ergonomic rather than aesthetic qualities. Small models may be made from cut and folded stiff paper, or any other material that does not require time-consuming techniques. Full-size prototypes can be assembled using anything from stiff cardboard through a wide selection of board materials to the materials intended for the final piece. Blocks of foam can be cut to give impressions of solid form but, as the project evolves and detailing becomes more refined, prototypes, if they are to have further value, must become equally refined. Thin legs, small feet and all other delicate elements must be represented accurately if they are to be useful in the appraisal of proportions. This is only viable with full-scale facsimiles since the precise nature of fine detailing cannot be reproduced, seen or assessed accurately

at anything less than full size. As in drawing, scaled details, particularly those at 1:5 or half-full size, are likely to give an impression of refinement that will not be delivered at full size. Where appearance only is being tested, the prototype need not have the load-bearing capabilities of the intended piece. Details can be represented in materials that are easier and more economical to work. Spray-painted wood can represent metal components convincingly. Multiple representations of joint and junction options can be made for critical comparison.

Developing the Prototype
Click Clack Chair – Nigel Coates Studio

This exercise was about refining proportions
and the relationship of components one to
the other. Full-size, freehand drawings were
easily and accurately made by tracing between
or around the mocked-up components.

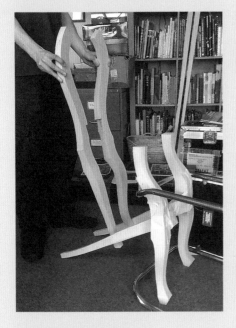

The principal components are loosely
assembled for initial appraisal.

The first prototype is assembled.

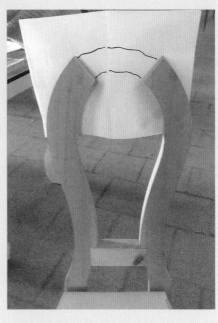

The profile of the missing component is agreed.

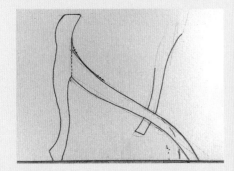

Above
Based on the evidence of the first prototype,
the final angles are committed to paper.

Right
The final prototype.

Far right
The final production piece – white version.

Production drawings

There is no room for ambiguity in production drawings. Established drawing conventions should be respected. Drawings should be as simple and therefore as comprehensible as possible. Well-resolved thinking will usually result in clarity of information. Drawings are made in a comfortable studio but may have to be interpreted and implemented in the confusion of a building site.

During both developmental and production drawing stages plans, elevations and sections should be made to a scale of at least 1:10, to establish the form and to identify areas requiring more detailed thought and representation. Details should be considered at as large a scale as is feasible, at least 1:5 but preferably 1:1. 1:2 can be misleading because it is large enough to suggest that one is looking at something full size and the outcome will therefore be assumed to be more delicate than it can be in reality. The computer allows the scale of a drawing to be constantly recalibrated. Investigation can be carried out at full size but the information transmitted at a more convenient scale.

In production drawings written information is as important as that drawn, which shows how components relate one to the other. Written notes specify details of their make-up. They should be brief, phrases rather than sentences, and purely factual. They are instructions to the maker, not explanations of aesthetic intention. They should make three factual statements. They should name the material or the object to which they refer; they should state its size and the method of fixing it. It is safe to assume that these three pieces of information should be added to every individual element within a detailed drawing. If one is unnecessary that will be evident. If additional information is required, this is likely to be less obvious and, for all details, the designer needs to visualize the process of assembly and decide if it is comprehensively, but concisely, described. It should then be obvious if something must be added.

The computer is the most efficient tool for conveying information to the maker. It allows perfect precision in the representation of the object. A drawing can be given clarity by the addition of tones. It makes the addition of dimensions and specification notes easier and allows changes and corrections to be made without physical damage to the drawing.

Whether made by hand or computer, the drawings that finally decide and communicate the essential information will be two-dimensional. Plans, elevations and sections, are the clearest and simplest way of conveying critical dimensions. It is however often useful to include three-dimensional views of the piece to clarify the final form that is defined by the two-dimensional conventions.

Production drawings must be intelligently ordered, numbered and cross-referenced. Plans and sections communicate the overview. They will show dimensions and general specification information, particularly of finishes. Details are frequently shown on another sheet. It is standard practice then to identify the location of that detailed condition on plan, section or both and to cross-reference it by giving it a unique identifying letter or number and citing the sheet number on which it will appear. For example, the location of a detail described as 'A' might be identified by circling it on a plan with an adjacent note saying 'see detail A on sheet 2'.

A completed set of production drawings will allow a maker to estimate the cost of the work and produce a 'tender', which is the estimated cost of all necessary work including labour and materials, the sum for which the maker is prepared to carry out the work. Frequently a number of makers, usually three, will be invited to tender with the contract being given to the one offering the lowest price. If the price is surprisingly low, the designer should check that the maker is capable of carrying out the work to a satisfactory standard. A surprisingly low tender may suggest miscalculation or an over-anxiety to get the work without necessarily having the financial resources to meet the demands of the contract adequately. Makers will frequently suggest simpler and cheaper ways of achieving a desired outcome and if the designer is confident that the result will be aesthetically acceptable and will meet practical demands, then there is every reason to accept the alternative offered. It is reasonable under these circumstances to ask makers to provide a guarantee of quality and, perhaps, a reduction in cost.

It is also common practice to select a single maker with appropriate specialist experience and ask for a quotation based on the production drawings. A better and more economical job is likely if makers are allowed to use the techniques best suited to their specialist machinery. They should then provide their own detailed production drawings and give copies to the designer for checking and approval before beginning fabrication. The maker will take responsibility for the practical performance of the work.

Sometimes changes must be made to a drawing after it has been issued, particularly where work is to be carried out on site and is subject to the complications that will arise as work progresses. Such changes should be described in an 'amendment' box on the relevant drawing, or drawings, be dated and given an identifying letter. The number of each amended sheet should then take on the letter or number of the last amendment as a suffix. For example a drawing originally numbered '3' with a latest amendment designated 'C' will take the revised number '3C'. The revised drawing should also be issued to all others whose work on site might be affected by the change and, in particular, the contractor responsible for the work on the site as a whole, if different from the maker, should be given a copy.

Not all amendments are dealt with formally. It may be enough to discuss and agree, verbally, a course of action but it is very likely that it will be more satisfactory to make quick, freehand, sketches to eliminate any ambiguity.

Often in early discussions with clients or specialist manufacturers the sketch will be the visual medium used to discuss an option or clarify something not adequately explained on a preliminary drawing. A spontaneous freehand sketch will frequently simplify and conclude a discussion. When discussing possibilities with a specialist, an exchange of sketches can become the backbone of the conversation. They do not need to have 'artistic' merit. Their role is to communicate facts.

Sketches need not necessarily be three-dimensional. Often plans and sections will provide a clearer explanation. It is important to concentrate on getting relative sizes and proportions of elements recognizably accurate.

Specifications and schedules

Any description of any design activity tends to focus on the visual component, the drawing and the model making, and to neglect the written component. The latter, however, particularly in interior design, is no less crucial in assuring final quality. Notes are as important as the drawn plans, sections and details that they augment, describing the materials to be used, the sizes of component parts, and the methods and techniques used in their assembly. They 'specify' the particularities of each element but the written specification goes beyond that, to prescribe the quality of bespoke pieces and the performance of those bought ready-made.

The general specification document will contain clauses that define standards of materials used, techniques for their assembly, and their performance after construction or installation. Designers may choose to insert their own clauses to ensure a particular outcome but most of the criteria will be those prescribed by the legislative or trade organizations for the country in which the work is to be carried out. Typical of these organizations are BSI (British Standards), DIN (German Institute for Standardization) and ANSI (American National Standards Institute). These bodies produce clauses that set out statutory requirements and each clause will be given a number that should be cited in a specification document. Work, such as the installation of electrical equipment, will be required to conform to the regulations set out by the relevant trade bodies.

This process takes potentially arduous liability away from a designer and gives it instead to suppliers and installers. It is, however, the designer's responsibility to identify the appropriate specification clauses. Some are generally applicable or relate to materials or activities used habitually and thus require no fresh research. Others will be project-specific and will need to be identified and their conditions understood.

Specification clauses, like drawings, become legal documents, part of the contract, agreed and signed by makers, contractors, suppliers and clients to ensure the quality and extent of work, and times of payment. They need to be clearly written, concise and concerned only with verifiable conditions. Various professional bodies issue standard clauses that should be incorporated in project-specific documents and clauses unique to the project should reproduce their style.

When designers select, or specify, ready-made furniture, they assume one of two roles. When there is a 'contractor', that is, a company carrying out the completion of all works, including supervising subcontractors responsible for specialist trades, the designer will issue the main contractor with a list, or 'schedule', setting out all the pieces of manufactured furniture to be included in the finished interior. The contractor will then be responsible for ordering, paying the supplier, organizing delivery to site, and installation or placement of the pieces and, for all these activities, will charge the client. Where work to the building's fabric is being carried out by a number of specialist contractors, none of whom has responsibility for the whole of the work, the designer will normally deal with the ordering of the specified pieces and charge the client for the service. If a designer pays for the pieces in the first instance, then the client will be billed and a percentage of the total cost added to cover the service.

Designers must always be concerned about the cost of projects, and when furniture forms a significant element in a budget the selection of pieces will be influenced by their financial impact on the project as a whole. Changing a first preference or negotiating with suppliers, who will normally reduce the unit cost for sizeable orders, is often necessary to make the whole project viable.

It is also useful to talk directly to suppliers of what is normally described as 'contract furniture'. These are companies who tend to specialize in furniture for a particular area of interior activity but most prolifically for the public and private office sector. It can be productive to talk to a number of suppliers about the general requirements, including the budget, for a particular project, and to invite them to make proposals, including costings, for those of their products that most effectively meet the specification. Companies are continually evolving new products and their representatives are familiar with the performance details of all items in their catalogue.

From Concept to Detail
Rogue Restaurant – LWD

The project begins with a site visit and an initial sketch that records the designer's first response to brief and building. Drawings become progressively more considered. As the materiality and detailing are resolved and the building becomes increasingly real in the designer's mind, so drawings become more technical. The complexity of a project cannot be properly understood or communicated by scribbles and sketches.

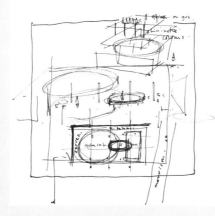

Above
A first, almost spontaneous record of strategic thinking made in a small sketchbook on a first visit to the site will often provide the foundation on which subsequent, more considered thinking can be built. The drawing is intended only for the designer and will mean little or nothing to anyone else.

Above
The uninterrupted line of the banquette's backrest expresses and emphasizes the line of the ellipse.

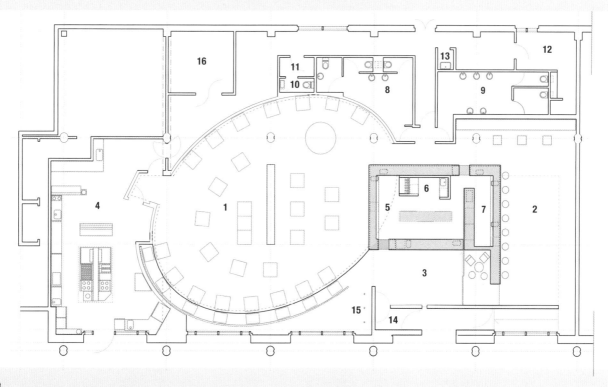

Above
The elliptical form from the first site sketch becomes the central public space; the utilitarian service areas remain, functionally four-square, around the perimeter. The spaces between them become interesting transitional spaces.

1	Restaurant.	6	Prep.
2	Bar.	7	Bar servery.
3	Kitchen.	8	Female WC.
4	Holding bar.	9	Male WC.
5	Restaurant servery.	10	Staff WC.
		11	Staff changing.

12	Office.
13	Cleaner's store.
14	Entrance lobby.
15	Cloakroom.
16	Plant room.

Below
Timber strips make a bar counter that is obsessively linear, in contrast to the soft curves of the restaurant plan.

Bottom
A section slides into another to provide staff access.

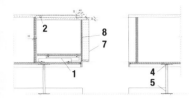
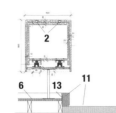
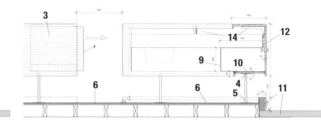

Section through bar with sliding pass

1   Häfele pull-out cupboard runner code 421.48.780.

2   35mm-/1¼in diameter nylon bearing.

3   Laminated sections of random oak, cherry, sycamore, ash, beech and elm make up the bar front and top.

4   M16 threaded rod to plate as adjustment to foot.

5   25mm/1in brushed stainless-steel leg threaded to 150mm-/6in-diameter fixing plate.

6   Dalsouple Uni Rubber flooring 'Fumée' fitted in accordance with manufacturer's instructions onto 25mm/1in marine ply deck screwed at 300mm/11¾in centres to 150 x 50mm/ 6 x 2in battens at 400mm/16¾in centres.

7   Telescopic bar pass-through.

8   Front face of ply finished with black laminate.

9   Stainless-steel worktop insert by specialist contractor.

10   25mm/1in marine ply biscuit jointed to solid timber bar.

11   Lafarge 'charcoal' *in situ* cast upstand by specialist contractor.

12   H&C water supply to sink to run behind stainless-steel upstand to work unit.

13   Rubber flooring to turn up into rebate in cast concrete upstand.

14   Häfele heavy-duty shelf support.

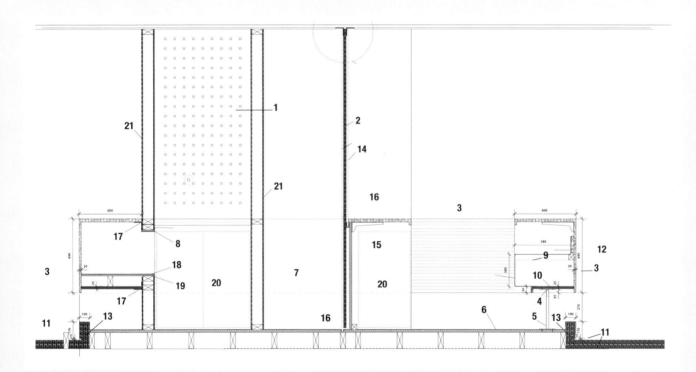

Section through bar and acrylic/fabric screen

1   Acrylic screen with stainless- steel rods as bottle rack.

2   Pleated fabric encased between acrylic panels.

3   Laminated sections of random, oak, cherry, sycamore, ash, beech and elm to make up bar front and top.

4   M16 threaded rod to plate as adjustment to foot.

5   25mm/1in brushed stainless-steel leg threaded to 150mm-/6in-diameter fixing plate.

6   Dalsouple Uni Rubber flooring 'Fumée' fitted in accordance with manufacturer's instructions onto 25mm/1in marine ply deck screw fixed at 300mm/11¾in centres to 150 x 50mm/6 x 2 in battens at 400mm/163¾in centres.

7   Telescopic bar pass-through.

8   12mm/½in black laminate-faced ply glued and screwed to trim opening. Stainless-steel screws to be countersunk and flush with surface at 400mm/16¾in centres on centre line of laminate.

9   Stainless-steel worktop insert by specialist contractor.

10   25mm/1in marine-ply biscuit jointed to solid timber bar.

11   Lafarge 'charcoal' *in situ* cast upstand by specialist contractor.

12   H&C water supply to sink to run behind stainless-steel upstand to work unit.

13   Rubber flooring to turn up into rebate in cast concrete upstand.

14   12mm/½in acrylic panels into stainless-steel channel at base and fixed with stainless-steel

machine screws into stainless-steel angle at head.

15   Häfele heavy-duty shelf support.

16   Stainless-steel channel.

17   75 x 4mm/3 x ¼in stainless-steel angle along length of bar run, screw-fixed with No. 75 x 5 stainless-steel screws at 400mm/16¾in centres.

18   15mm/½in black laminate-faced ply with laminate lip as shelf for glasses cupboard.

19   SRL 6 shadow line reveal to plasterboard.

20   Space for two-door chiller.

21   12.5mm/5in moisture-resistant plasterboard fixed to 100 x 50mm/4 x 2in studs at 600mm/23½in centres.

Glossary

Acrylic
In furniture design normally refers to acrylic glass, a transparent thermoplastic derived from Poly (methyl methacrylate). The generic name for products such as Plexiglas, Lucite and Perspex.

Adhesives
A liquid or semi-liquid that bonds items together. Adhesives cure or harden by either evaporating a solvent or by chemical reactions between two or more constituents. A specified adhesive must be suitable for the materials being bonded.

Aggregate
A collection of items gathered together to form a total quantity. In interior and furniture design it usually refers to aggregate data combined from several measurements.

Ambulant
From the Latin for 'walking'. In interior and furniture design 'ambulant disabled' is used to describe someone who is not wheelchair-bound but will have some impairment of movement that a designer should take account of in the development of spaces and furniture.

ANSI (American National Standards Institute)
A not-for-profit organization that oversees the development of voluntary consensus standards for products and services in the US and coordinates with international standards, allowing US products to be sold worldwide.

Anthropometric
From the Greek meaning 'measurement of man', it refers to the measurement of the human individual.

Armature
The framework around which a piece of furniture is built. Usually made of timber or mild steel, it provides structure and stability for softer or more malleable materials such as fabric or plastics.

Batch production
A technique used in manufacturing where an object is created stage-by-stage over a number of workstations. It often describes items made in quantities greater than a single 'one-off' but less than in high-investment, high-volume mass-production.

Bespoke
Describes an item made to a client's specification or to fit a specific space.

Biodegradable
Used to describe materials that dissolve chemically by bacterial or other biological means.

Bodging
A traditional wood-turning craft, using green (unseasoned) wood, normally to manufacture chairs.

BS (British Standard)
The formal consensus of standards developed by the BSI Group under a Royal Charter for products, materials and services produced in the UK.

Cable management
The design and control of the cable runs to electrical equipment, usually on a desk or workstation but can refer to cable runs within an interior.

CAD (Computer-aided design)
The use of computer systems and programs to assist in the creation, modification, analysis or optimization of design.

CAM (Computer-aided manufacture)
The integration of computer-aided design and computer numerically controlled manufacturing tools.

Cantilever
A beam anchored at only one end. Cantilevered construction allows for overhanging or projected structures without external bracing.

Casting
A manufacturing process by which a liquid material is poured into a mould of the desired finished shape.

Chipboard
Board manufactured from wood chips with a synthetic resin or suitable binder, which is then pressed and extruded. Cheaper than conventional plywood, it is used when appearance or strength are less important than cost. It deteriorates if it comes into contact with moisture. Also known as particleboard.

Cladding
The covering of one material with another, usually a finishing material such as timber attached to a structural frame.

CNC (Computer Numerically Controlled)
Numerical control is the operation of a machine tool abstractly through commands encoded on a storage medium rather than manually.

Contractor
A person or company that undertakes a contract to provide a service or job, in interior design usually the construction and building element of the contract.

Datum
A standard position or level from which measurements are taken. The fixed point from which running dimensions would be taken when making a survey of an interior.

Digital design
A design process that involves the use of computer drawing programs.

DIN (*Deutsches Institut für Normung*)
German national standards body recognized by the German government.

Electrostatic
Describes the build-up of a charge on the surface of objects. 'Electrostatic induction' is used in commercial applications such as industrial painting systems for the economical and even application of enamel and polyurethane paints.

Ergonomics
The 'fit' between the user, equipment and their environment.

Fibreoptic
Optical fibre made of glass (silica) or plastic about the thickness of a human hair that acts as a 'light pipe' to transmit light between two ends of the fibre. In interiors, fibreoptics are mainly used in lighting, particularly in exhibition display, where the light source and any potential heat can be kept away from delicate objects. They can also be hidden in materials such as concrete, only becoming visible as points of light when needed.

Figure
The pattern of grain on a piece of timber.

Fluorescent
In a fluorescent lamp or tube electricity excites mercury atoms, producing short-wave ultraviolet light that then causes a phosphor to fluoresce, producing visible light. The luminous efficacy of a compact fluorescent lamp is about four times that of an incandescent bulb.

Flush
Completely level or even with another surface.

Freestanding
In an interior, an object or item of furniture that does not rely on the building structure for support.

Galvanizing
The process of applying a protective zinc coating to steel or iron, either with an electro-chemical process or more commonly in hot-dip galvanizing where steel parts are submerged in a bath of molten zinc.

Gasket
A mechanical seal that fills the space between two joining surfaces, usually to prevent leakage from or into the joined objects.

Geotextiles
Permeable fabrics typically made from polypropylene or polyester, normally used as a filter or separating fabric against soil.

Grain
The pattern of a piece of timber caused by the fibres that run along its length. A piece of timber will be strongest along its grain and weakest across it.

Hardwood
In temperate climates, wood usually of broad-leaved or deciduous trees but in the tropics and subtropics mostly from evergreens. Hardwoods are not always harder than softwoods: balsa, for instance, is a hard wood while yew is a soft wood.

Housing
A slot cut into the surface of a piece of wood to take another piece; it is cut across the grain rather than parallel to it (which would be a groove). In the US and Canada called a 'dado'.

Joist
A horizontal supporting member that runs from wall to wall to support a ceiling, roof or floor.

Laminate
The technique of manufacturing a material in multiple layers so that the strength of the composite material is improved. Plywood is a common example.

Laminated glass
Commonly made by laminating a tough plastic between two sheets of glass. If broken, the glass will be held together by the plastic, minimizing the risk of injury from sharp fragments. Also known as safety glass.

LED (light emitting diode)
A semi-conductor light source where electrons release energy in the form of photons in an effect called electroluminescence. Modern, high-efficiency LEDs are used in lighting interiors. Replacing incandescent bulbs with LEDs can reduce a building's carbon footprint by 85 per cent.

Marquetry
The art of applying pieces of veneer, usually timber, to a surface to form decorative patterns, designs or pictures.

Masonry
The building of structures from individual units bonded by a mortar; can also refer to the individual units themselves, commonly made from brick, stone or concrete.

Mass production
The large-scale production of a standardized product, usually on an assembly line.

MDF (Medium-density fibreboard)
The generic name for any dry-process fibreboard where wood fibres are combined with a wax and resin binder to form panels by applying high temperature and pressure. It is far more uniform than natural wood but is liable to swell when it comes into contact with moisture. Formaldehyde resins commonly used in the manufacture of MDF may be emitted as urea-formaldehyde, so the edges of MDF should be sealed to protect the health of users.

Neoprene
A synthetic rubber produced by the polymerization of chloroprene often used as a spacer or gasket as it resists degradation better than natural rubber; also the material favoured for laptop sleeves and tablet holders.

Organic
Of, or pertaining to, an organism; an organic material would be one that has come from a living entity such as timber from a tree. 'Organic architecture' stresses interrelatedness combining site, buildings, furnishings and surroundings into a unified whole. As a design philosophy, it could simply mean echoing the patterns and forms found in living systems.

OSB (Orientated strand board)
A particle board formed by layering shavings of wood in specific directions that are then compressed and bonded with a wax and synthetic resin. Also known as 'Sterling board' in the UK and Ireland and as 'Aspenite' in the US and Canada.

Oxidation
A reaction between one oxygen atom and one other element. To a designer the most common example of oxidation would be the development of rust on iron or on its alloys such as steel.

Panel
Usually a flat and thin piece of wood or glass set into a frame. Plywood or composites such as MDF or OSB are referred to as panel products as they fulfil this function.

PAR (Planed all round)
Of timber, converted from a log into long, rectangular sections and put through a planer to smooth its surface.

Perforated
Describes a material with small holes that can be part of a pattern over the whole surface for decoration or to let light or air through, or a series of holes designed to allow a material to be torn or folded along a precise line.

Plastics
There are two types of plastic: thermoplastic and thermosetting polymers. Thermoplastics such as polyethylene and polypropylene do not undergo a chemical change in their composition when heated and can be remoulded. Thermosetting plastics once melted and hardened remain solid and cannot be reformed. Most plastics are derived from petrochemicals but concerns about CO_2 emissions have lead to the development of bio-plastics from plant materials such as starch and cellulose.

Plinth
In architecture a plinth is the base or platform on which a column or structure rests; in interiors it is most commonly the recessed base to a desk or kitchen unit.

Plywood
A manufactured wood panel made from thin veneers of wood layered at right angles to one another for strength and stability.

Powder coating
A finish typically applied electrostatically as a dry powder (either thermoplastic or thermosetting polymer) that is then cured under heat. Powder coating is used to give a finish to metals and alloys such as steel and aluminium but it is also possible to powder coat materials such as MDF.

Prefabrication
The practice of assembling components or complete structures 'off site' in a factory and delivering the structures to the site completely assembled.

Prototype
An early sample or model of a design idea to test how a product or structure will function and fulfil its brief.

Recycling
The process of reusing materials in new products to avoid waste and the consumption of new materials. It differs from re-use, where a material such as a brick or steel beam is used in the original form. Designing for reuse is more sustainable than designing for recycling.

Refurbish
To renovate or redecorate a building or interior space, usually to redefine the space with a contemporary aesthetic or to give a new function. It differs from 'restoration' where the interior would be repaired and preserved in its original form.

Rib
In interior and furniture design, a structural element, usually a strip of plywood or timber fixed at right angles as a stiffener to a thinner panel material.

Sandblasting
Roughening, shaping or removing contaminates from a surface by firing a stream of fine sand under pressure. Different abrasives can be used in similar processes such as bead blasting, grit blasting and shot blasting.

Scale
A scale model or drawing is a representation of an object or space larger or smaller than its actual size while maintaining relative proportions.

Schedule
Usually a list or inventory of items or finishes stating their position and quantity within an interior.

Seasoning
The controlled drying of timber to reduce the impact of dimensional changes and shrinkage. Ideally the moisture content of timber would be reduced to humidity levels relative to where it is eventually to be used. Air drying takes about one year per 25mm or 1" of thickness; kiln drying, where timber is stacked in chambers and heat is introduced, is a quicker and more controlled process. Some timbers such as beech take on a different colour tone when kiln dried as opposed to air dried.

Socket
A recess into which something else will fit or revolve; or an electrical socket that receives a plug or a light bulb.

Softwood
Gynosperm trees such as conifers; most evergreen trees are softwood. Most of the world's timber production is softwood as fast-growing trees such as spruce and pine supply the building trade with structural timber for framework.

Specification
Precise description or identification of a feature normally on a working drawing or written specification document that specifies the standard of workmanship and materials required in a piece of work.

Splashback
A protective panel at the back of a work surface in a kitchen or bar that prevents damage to a more vulnerable wall surface.

Stain

A colourant in a suspension agent such as water or alcohol, or a finish such as shellac, lacquer or varnish usually used on timber. Unlike opaque paint, stain allows the figure or grain of the timber to be visible

Steel

An alloy of iron that has been through a process where the carbon content of 'iron ore' or raw iron has been reduced and impurities such as sulphur and phosphorus and alloying elements such as magnesium, nickel and chromium have been added. Varying the quantities of alloys controls the steel's hardness and tensile strength.

Surface-mounted

Fixed to a wall or desktop surface and therefore visible, as opposed to 'ducted' behind a wall or other surface and hidden.

Suspension

Usually refers to the hanging of an object from the structure of a building or within a structure designed for the purpose.

Sustainability

The capacity of an object or process to endure; but more widely used to mean its lifetime capacity to have minimal effect upon the Earth's resources. In 1978 the UN's Brundtland Commission defined sustainable development as that which 'meets the needs of the present without compromising the ability of future generations to meet their own needs'. For a designer this means not only looking at the embodied energy and creation of CO_2 in the production of objects but recognising the greater problem of finite resources. Some materials, such as timber, can be replaced at the same rate as it is used, others, such as mined minerals and oils, are finite and will eventually run out. Designers should both choose materials carefully and design for re-use or at least recycling of materials.

Terrazzo

A composite material of chips of marble quartz granite, glass or other suitable chips sprinkled onto a concrete or epoxy resin finish which when cured or dry is then ground smooth and polished. Used as a floor or wall treatment.

Textiles

Flexible woven materials of natural or artificial fibres formed by weaving, knitting, knotting or pressing fibres together.

Thread

Usually refers to a 'screw thread' the helical ridge cut around a screw or bolt.

Turning

A machining process where a material such as wood, metal or plastic is rotated on a lathe and a cutting tool is held against it, either manually or controlled via a CNC program.

Underlay

A thin layer of material such as rubber or foam laid beneath carpeting or other floor covering to provide insulation against sound or moisture, or to prevent cracks in floorboards becoming visible.

Upholstery

The work of providing furniture with padding, springs, webbing and then coverings such as fabric or leather.

Varnish

A transparent, hard, protective finish primarily used on wood; traditionally a combination of a drying oil, a resin and a thinner.

Veneer

Usually refers to wood veneer, thin slices of wood normally thinner than 3mm glued onto core panels.

Washer

A thin plate usually of metal or plastic with a hole, normally used to spread the load between the bolt and a nut and the material being fastened; a washer can also be used as a spacer.

Webbing

A strong, woven fabric used mostly in upholstery.

Welding

Usually refers to a fabrication method for joining metals with molten solder but can be used for thermoplastics where the junctions of the materials to be joined are melted and a molten filler material (the weld pool) is added that cools to make a strong joint.

Further reading

Architectural Woodwork Standards, 1st Edition, Architectural
Woodwork Institute, 2009

Ballard Bell, Victoria & Rand, Patrick, *Materials for Architectural
Design*, Laurence King Publishing, 2006
ISBN: 1-850669-480-1

Braungart, Michael & McDonough, William, *Cradle to Cradle:
Remaking the Way We Make Things*, Vintage, 2009
ISBN 978-0-099-53547-8

Fiell, Charlotte & Peter, *1000 Chairs*, Taschen 2005
ISBN 3-8228-7965-7

Lefteri, Chris, *Making It: Manufacturing Techniques for Product
Design*, Laurence King Publishing Ltd, 2012
ISBN: 13-978-1-85669-506-0

Lefteri, Chris, *Materials for Inspirational Design*, Rotovision, 2006
ISBN: 13978-2-940361-50-2

Lovell, Sophie, *Furnish: Furniture and Interior Design for the 21st
Century*, Die Gestalten Verlag GmbH & Co, 2007
ISBN: 978-3-89955-176-1

Lovell, Sophie, *Limited Edition: Prototypes, One Offs and Design Art
Furniture*, Birkhuaser Verlag AG, 2009
ISBN 978-3-7643-8895

Simpson, Chris, *The Essential Guide to Woodwork*, Thunder Bay
Press, 2002
ISBN 1-57145-819-0

Thompson, Rob, *Prototyping and Low-volume Production*, Thames
& Hudson, 2011
ISBN 9780500289181

Websites

http://www.vitra.com
http://www.designboom.com
http://architonic.com
http://www.materialconnexion
http://www.dezeen.com

Index

Picture credits

1 Karim Rashid, photo Lukas Roth. 3 Karim Rashid, photo Lukas Roth. 5t Wunderteam, photo Olo Rutkowsk, Ula Tarasiewicz; b Graven Images, photo Renzo Mazzolini. 6 Istockphoto/ helovi. 7l Official White House Photostream/photo Pete Souza; r Istockphoto.com/ Ljupco. 8l Scala, Florence; r Digital image © 2013, The Museum of Modern Art/Scala, Florence. 9 Oskar Zieta, Zieta Prozessdesign. 10 and 11 XM3, photography Paulina Sasinowska. 12tl Ravenshoe Group/Flickr creative commons; tr Accreation Disc/Flickr creative commons; bl Sunshine City / Flickr creative commons; br Yatuka Tsutano /Flickr creative commons. 13 Drew Plunkett. 14 Philip Watts Design. 15t and bl Vitra, photography Marc Eggimann; br Vitra, photography Giovanna Silva for Abitare. 16 UXUS, photo Dim Balsem. 18 Kretyen/Flickr creative commons. 21 and 22 Brinkworth, photo Louise Melchior. 23l Eva Jiricna Architects, photo Richard Bryant; r Eva Jiricna Architects, photo Peter Paige. 24–25 March Studio. 26–27 Stad, photo Hiroshi Mizusaki. 28tl Tokujin Yoshioka, photo courtesy of designer; tr APA, photo Nick Hufton; bl Guise, photo Jesper Lindstrom. 29 Dear Design, photo Jonathan Richards Picture Studios Ltd. 30 Tokujin Yoshioka, photo Koji Fijii (Nacasa & Partners Inc.). 31 Graven Images, photo Renzo Mazzolini. 32 Destilat Architecture and Design. 34 Nomad RDC, photo John Cooper. 37 Nomad RDC, photo Antonio Tammaro. 38 Nomad RDC, photography Antonio Tammaro. 40 and 41 El Ultimo Grito. 42b Tim Venke/ Jouke Anema. 43t Drew Plunkett; c Graven Images, photo Renzo Mazzolini; b Tim Venke. 44 Rosan Bosch & Rune Fjord, photo Anders Sune Berg. 45t Origins Architects, photo Stijn Poelstra. 46 Graven Images, photo Renzo Mazzolini. 47l Vonsung, photo Joseph Sung and Teresa Wong; r Arka Design, photo Paul Zanre. 48 Karim Rashid, photo Lukas Roth. 49t NHDRU, photo Derryk Menere; b Karim Rashid, photo Lukas Roth. 50 Ab Rogers Design. 51t Francesc Rife Studio, photo Fernando Alda; b NHDRU, photo Derryk Menere. 52l RARE Architecture, photo Edmund Sumner; r Jestico +Whiles, photo Ales Jungmann. 53 Ab Rogers Design. 54 Nigel Coates. 55t MSB Estudi-taller d'arquitectura I disseny, photo Miquel Merce; b Graven Images, photo Renzo Mazzolini. 56 Karim Rashid, photo Jean-François Jassaud 57 Graven Images, photo Renzo Mazzolini. 58–59 Ben Kelly Design, photo Steve Reynolds. 60tl and tr Outline, photo Philip Vile; b Ben Kelly Design, photo Alan Forbes. 61t SAQ; b Wunderteam, photo Olo Rutkowski, Ula Tarasiewicz. 64–65 UXUS, photos Dim Balsem. 66t Serie Architects Mumbai, photo Fram Petit; b Graven Images, photo G1. 67t Karim Rashid, photo Renzo Mazzolini; b Graven Images, photo Renzo Mazzolini. 68 Outline, photo Philip Vile. 70l Eva Jiricna Architects, photo Richard Bryant; r Drew Plunkett. 71 Drew Plunkett. 72 Nick Coombe Architecture, photo James Morris. 74–77 Ben Kelly Design, photography Philip Vile. 78–79 Arka Design, photography Artan Sherifi. 80 photo Drew Plunkett. 82 and 83t Graven Images, photography Renzo Mazzolini. 86–87 El Ultimo Grito. 88 Nomad RDC, photo Antonio Tammaro. 90 Graven Images, photo Renzo Mazzolini. 91 Stanley Saitowitz/Natoma Architects, photo Rien van Rijthoven. 95 Drew Plunkett. 96 Zaha Hadid, photo Luke Hayes, luke@lukehayes.com. 98 Vitra. 99 Digital image © 2013, The Museum of Modern Art/ Scala, Florence. 100t Soho House; b Claesson Koivisto Rune Architects, photo Ate E:son Lindman. 101t Vitra; bl yisris.Flickr creative commons; br Drew

Plunkett. 102 Sam Booth. 103tl Joyce Porte, photo Drew Plunkett; tr Drew Plunkett; b Lindsay Taylor, photo Drew Plunkett. 104tl Martin Kaltwasser/Folke Kobberling photo Brian Benson; tr Karla Otto; b Karla Otto. 105tl Brinkworth, photo Louise Melchor; tr Studio Mammink & Bey, photo Mammink & Bey; bl Aekae, photo Nico Scharer; br Sruli Recht. 106tl Scalar Architecture, photo Kris Tamburello; tr Elding Oscarson, photo Ake E:son Lindman; b Conservatorium Hotel Amsterdam, arch. Lissoni Associati, photo Amit Geron. 107t Uxus Design. 108 SAQ. 109t EFGH, photo Kelly Shimoda; bl Karim Rashid; br Katrin Greiling. 110tl Zaha Hadid/ Patrik Schumacher; tr Zaha Hadid/photo Gavin Jackson/arcaid. co.uk; b Zaha Hadid/Patrik Schumacher. 111 Zaha Hadid/Patrick Schumacher. 112l TJEP, photo courtesy TJEP; r Softroom, photo Nikolas Koenig. 113tl Gitta Gschwendtner/photo Ed Reeve; tr Carl Clerkin/photo Ed Reeve; bl and br Rory Dodd designers block. 114-15 Sam Booth. 116 Danny Lane, photography Peter Wood. 118 SAQ. 119 Guise, photo Jesper Lindstrom. 120t Gre West/Flickr creative commons; b Jeroen Verhoeven. 121 Asa Ashuach Studio. 122 Sam Booth. 127A Jerszy Seymore; B and C Christof Schmidt/photo Ali Schmidt; D Christof Schmidt; E Elise Gabriel for the Green Factory; F Bakery Design; G and H Elise Gabriel for the Green Factory. 128 Nicola Zocca. 129 Toby Wintheringham. 130-31 Danny Lane, photography Peter Wood. 133l Sam Booth, photography Ewan Anderson; r Sam Booth. 134 Sam Booth. 135 Jennings/Jordanhill School. 136l Sam Booth/ John Crosby; r Sam Booth. 137 Sam Booth/John Crosby. 138 Jennings/ Jordanhill School. 139t Maurice Mentjens, photo Leon Abraas; l Francesc Rife Studio, photo Fernandi Alda; r MSB Estudi-taller d'arquitectura i disseny, photo Miquel Merce. 140r Sam Booth. 141A-E Kelwood Engineering; F Jennings/Jordanhill School. 142 A-C Danny Lane; D Danny Lane, photography Peter Wood. 143 Bakery /Gilli Kuchik, Ran Amitai. 144tl and bl Vrtiska-Zak, photo Filip Slapal; br Francesco Moncada, photo Alberto Moncada. 145l Sam Booth; r Ralston & Bau, photo Vincent Baillais. 146 Sam Booth, photography Ewan Adamson. 147tl and bl Eight Inch Ltd; r Maison Martin Margiela. 148 Eva Jiricna Architects, photo Richard Bryant. 149 Danny Lane, photography Peter Wood. 150t Thomas Heatherwick; bl and br Thomas Heatherwick/ c Angle Monzon 151t Sam Booth; bl and br Sam Booth /John Crosbie. 152 El Ultimo Grito. 153t Sam Booth; bl Peter Holmes; br Joe Lodge/Flickr creative commons. 154t El Ultimo Grito; tr and cr Bakery/ Gilli Kuchik, Ran Amitai; b El Ultimo Grito. 155tl Jestico + Whiles, photo Ales Jungmann; r Marcel Wanders Studio, photo Marcel Wanders; bl Mancini Enterprises Pvt. Ltd, photo Mancini Enterprises. 166 Sam Booth/ Dave Ramsden. 169A and B Sam Booth; C Sam Booth/ Jenny Booth; D Sam Booth/ Tom Booth. 171 Sam Booth. 173 Nigel Coates Studio. 174 MUMA. 175 ECA Interior design deparment. 176 Nigel Coates Studio. 179 Sam Booth. 180 Sam Booth/John Crosbie. 181 Sam Booth.

Acknowledgements

Sam Booth would like to thank Maggie, Tom and Jenny.

This project is dedicated to Nicola Zocca.